40 Sho

CORNWALL

Produced by AA Publishing
© AA Media Limited 2011

Researched and written by
Des Hannigan

Additional material and walks
by Des Hannigan (updated by Martin
Dunning, Des Hannigan and Sue Viccars)

Commissioning Editor: David Popey
Series Management: Sandy Draper
Series Design: Tracey Butler
Copy-editor: Chris Bagshaw
Proofreader: Pam Stagg
Picture Researcher: Alice Earle
Internal Repro and Image Manipulation:
Sarah Montgomery
Cartography provided by the Mapping
Services Department of AA Publishing
Production: Lorraine Taylor

Published by AA Publishing (a trading name
of AA Media Limited, whose registered office
is Fanum House, Basing View, Basingstoke,
Hampshire RG21 4EA; registered number
06112600)

  This product
includes mapping
data licensed from the Ordnance Survey®
with the permission of the Controller of
Her Majesty's Stationery Office. © Crown
Copyright 2011. All rights reserved.
Licence number 100021153.

A04616

978-0-7495-6901-3
978-0-7495-6913-6 (SS)

Colour separation by AA Digital

Printed by Oriental Press

Visit AA Publishing at theAA.com/shop

A CIP catalogue record for this book is
available from the British Library.

The contents of this book are believed
correct at the time of printing. Nevertheless,
the publishers cannot be held responsible
for any errors or omissions or for changes
in the details given in this book or for
the consequences of any reliance on the
information it provides. This does not affect
your statutory rights. We have tried to
ensure accuracy in this book, but things do
change and we would be grateful if readers
would advise us of any inaccuracies they
may encounter.

We have taken all reasonable steps to ensure
that these walks are safe and achievable
by walkers with a realistic level of fitness.
However, all outdoor activities involve a
degree of risk and the publishers accept
no responsibility for any injuries caused to
readers whilst following these walks. For
more advice on walking safely see page 144.
The mileage range shown on the front cover
is for guidance only – some walks may be
less than or exceed these distances.

Some of the walks may appear in other AA
books and publications.

Picture credits

The Automobile Association would like
to thank the following photographers,
companies and picture libraries for their
assistance in the preparation of this book.

3 AA/Adam Burton; 7 AA/John Wood; 10
AA/Jon Wyand; 17 AA/John Wood; 30-31
AA/John Wood; 50-51 Gary Eastwood
Photography/Alamy; 64 AA/John Wood; 74
Vince Bevan/Alamy; 82 Roger Hollingsworth/
Alamy; 100 AA/John Wood; 107 AA/Adam
Burton; 114 AA/John Wood; 128 AA/John
Wood; 140 AA/Roger Moss.

Every effort has been made to trace the
copyright holders, and we apologise in
advance for any accidental errors. We would
be happy to apply the corrections in the
following edition of this publication.

Opposite: Priest's Cove, Cape Cornwall

40 Short Walks in

CORNWALL

Contents

Rating
Each walk is rated for its relative difficulty compared to the other walks in this book. Walks marked ✚⊹⊹ are likely to be shorter and easier with little total ascent. The hardest walks are marked ✚✚✚

Walking in Safety
For advice and safety tips see page 144.

Introduction

Cornwall's narrow peninsula runs westwards from the banks of the River Tamar for nearly 100 miles (161km) until it gives way to the Atlantic at the rocky fist of Land's End, the ancient Belerion of the Roman chroniclers. This is where England begins and ends, although the Cornish often dispute the English connection, so geographically independent and 'different' is this sea-girt peninsula that is washed by the mighty Atlantic on one side and by the gentler English Channel on the other. Cornwall is a repository of deep-seated traditions and a distinctively 'Celtic' culture that have given the county a unique character to match its unique topography.

Spectacular Coastline

Vast rocky headlands protrude into the sea along Cornwall's corrugated coastline. They are buttressed with spectacular cliffs and pierced by deep zawns, those dark narrow ravines that echo with the roar of the sea and the strident call of seabirds. Sweeping panoramas unfold to either side. There are gentler interruptions where lush valleys run down to rocky coves or to beaches of golden sand, while picturesque old fishing villages and resort towns add variety to the mix. This book offers a selection of walks that explore some of Cornwall's finest stretches of coast, from the breezy flower-swathed cliff tops at Bude to the tree-shrouded shores of the Helford River and the Fal Estuary, from the fearsome cliffs of the Land's End peninsula to the gentler Fowey coast. Every day is rewarding, regardless of the time of year; at best when the golden light spills from a blue sky, yet still exhilarating in brisk and boisterous weather.

A Walker's Paradise

Cornwall's coast is a paradise for the walker, but the inland areas of the county have much to offer, too. There are no vast open spaces here to match those of Devon's Dartmoor, but the long dragon's back of granite that wriggles down the length of Cornwall, from Bodmin Moor to Land's End, supports pockets of high moorland. The walks here pass through landscapes that are peppered with standing stones and burial chambers of the Bronze and Iron ages, matched by the ruins of Cornwall's famous Victorian tin and copper mines. Some inland walks wind through deep woodland, as at Cardinham and Lerryn. Others take you through the heart of archetypal Cornish villages and towns, including the larger centres of Truro and Penzance whose architecture matches anywhere in the West Country for style and character.

Opposite: Coverack, Lizard Peninsula

All of the walks described in this book are circular and follow rights of way, permissive paths or short lengths of public road. Today, the National Trust cares for numerous sections of the Cornish coast and, in many cases, it is because of the Trust's good work that permissive footpaths can be used to close the circle, while Trust car parks make for convenient access. Other permissive paths are routed across fields in keeping with environmental farming agreements and much maintenance work and signposting of footpaths is carried out by Cornwall Council. With its remarkable coast, its lonely moors and deep woods, Cornwall rewards those who are willing to explore on foot beyond popular destinations. Best boot forward therefore through the inspiring landscapes of this fabulous first-and-last peninsula.

Using the Book

This collection of 40 walks is easy to use. Use the locator map to select your walk, then turn to the map and directions of your choice. The route of each walk is shown on a map and clear directions help you follow the walk. Each route is accompanied by background information about the walk and area.

INFORMATION PANELS

An information panel for each walk details the total distance, landscape, paths, parking, public toilets and any special conditions that apply, such as restricted access or level of dog friendliness. The minimum time suggested for the walk is for reasonably fit walkers and doesn't allow for stops.

ASCENT AND DIFFICULTY

An indication of the gradients you will encounter is shown by the rating ▲▲▲ (no steep slopes) to ▲▲▲ (several very steep slopes). Walks are also rated for difficulty. Walks marked ✚✚✚ are likely to be shorter and easier with little total ascent. The hardest walks are marked ✚✚✚.

MAPS AND START POINTS

There are 40 maps covering the walks. Some walks have a suggested option in the same area. Each walk has a suggested Ordnance Survey map. The start of each walk is given as a six-figure grid reference prefixed by two letters indicating which 100km square of the National Grid it refers to. You'll find more information on grid references on most Ordnance Survey maps.

CAR PARKING

Many of the car parks suggested are public, but occasionally you may find you have to park on the roadside or in a lay-by. Please be considerate when you leave your car, ensuring that access roads or gates are not blocked and that other vehicles can pass safely.

DOGS

We have tried to give dog owners useful advice about how dog friendly each walk is. Please respect other countryside users. Keep your dog under control, especially around livestock, and obey local bylaws and other dog control notices. Remember, it is against the law to let your dog foul in public areas, especially in villages and towns.

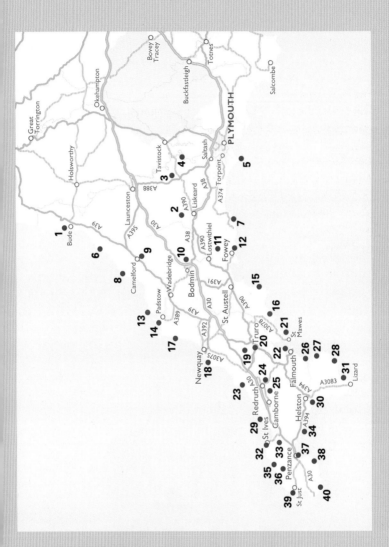

KEY TO WALKING MAPS

→→	Walk Route	▦	Built-up Area
❶	Route Waypoint	▦	Woodland Area
– – –	Adjoining Path	👫	Toilet
⧹ǀ⧸	Viewpoint	P	Car Park
•	Place of Interest	🛏	Picnic Area
⌂	Steep Section	)(	Bridge

A WILD FLOWER FIESTA AT BUDE

A stroll through coastal heathland where the cliff edges provide a refuge for countless wild flowers.

The grassy coastline north of Bude looks more like a golf course than a wild landscape. Yet this is wild country all the same, where the ground ends at the edge of steep cliffs. You might think it an unlikely haven for wild flowers, but these windy, salt-scoured acres are a valuable refuge for resilient maritime plants. In spring and early summer especially, this is a walk for the wildflower aficionado as much as it is a delightful outing in itself. Most of the area through which the walk passes is cared for by the National Trust.

Grasslands

In spring the dominant wild flower on these cliffs is the spring squill, while other plants to look for are lilac-coloured scurvy grass, pink thrift and white sea campion. By July the ground is dense with the yellow and orange flowers of kidney vetch and the pink and white florets of the aromatic wild carrot.

The cliffs are swathed in vegetation and look like the tumbling waves of a green sea. You can see this in places where the coast path skirts the edges of Maer Cliff and crosses above Furzey Cove, the site of a huge landslip. The cliffs here vary from vertical walls of scabrous and very unstable rock to easier angled sheets of rippled slabs where groups practice abseiling. At Northcott Mouth the cliffs give way to a wide stony beach pocked with rock pools.

Old Bridleway

From Northcott Mouth, the second leg of the walk follows the line of an old bridleway and then veers off through an area of woodland, a profound contrast to the open breezy acres of Maer Cliff. Beneath trees such as beech, alder, Scots pine and Corsican pine, look out for primroses and daffodils in early spring. Even the tall yellow flag iris thrives in such a moist environment. The last section of the walk leads you past the Maer Lake Nature Reserve, a large area of wetland that is flooded in winter. There is no public access to the area from the roadside but you can get an excellent view of the many birds. These may include snipe, spoonbill, wild geese and whooper swans. Bring your binoculars!

Opposite: A family paddle in the sea at Bude

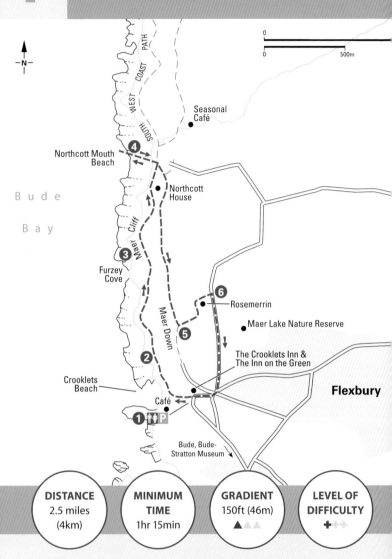

DISTANCE	MINIMUM TIME	GRADIENT	LEVEL OF DIFFICULTY
2.5 miles (4km)	1hr 15min	150ft (46m) ▲▲▲	+++

PATHS Excellent throughout; 3 stiles **LANDSCAPE** Coastal cliffs. In places, the grassy cliff top ends very sharply above high cliffs. You should keep well back from the cliff edge **SUGGESTED MAPS** OS Explorer 111 Bude, Boscastle & Tintagel and 126 Clovelly & Hartland **START/FINISH** Grid reference: SS 204071 **DOG FRIENDLINESS** Dogs on lead through grazed areas **PARKING** Crooklets Beach car park. Follow signs for Crooklets. Large pay-and-display car park that can be very busy in summer **PUBLIC TOILETS** Crooklets Beach

WALK 1 DIRECTIONS

1 From Crooklets Beach car park, go towards the beach, turn right and cross a wooden bridge and then head diagonally left to climb steps. Pass behind some beach huts, then turn left along a stony track between walls. Go up more steps and follow the coast path, signposted 'Maer Cliff'.

2 There are a number of path options ahead. The direct route follows a broad and direct grassy track, but you can follow other obvious paths closer to the cliff edge, but always with great care. Far ahead you can see the satellite communication dishes of Morwenstow.

3 Follow the cliff edge path towards a white bungalow-style building, Northcott House. Bear round right alongside the house and then turn left through a gate onto a rough track. Bear off left along a narrow path just beyond the entrance to Northcott House. Follow the path down to Northcott Mouth beach.

✐ IN THE AREA

Go for a swim from Bude's splendid beach, but pay close attention to Lifeguard warning flags. Have a stroll round busy Bude itself and visit the Bude-Stratton Museum, located in the old blacksmith's forge on the Lower Wharf of the Bude Canal. The canal was established in the early 19th century, originally to transport calcium-rich sand to inland farms as fertiliser.

---

4 Retrace your steps from the beach area towards Northcott House and go along the track behind the house. Go through the gate met previously. Keep straight ahead along a broad stony track. Ignore a high slate stile on your left and keep straight ahead through a wide gap by the end of a high wall.

🍴 EATING AND DRINKING

There are a number of beachside cafés at Crooklets Beach. Just opposite the Crooklets car park entrance are The Crooklets Inn and The Inn On The Green, both serving snacks, pub lunches and full meals. There is a seasonal café in a caravan at Northcott Mouth.

---

5 Go left and over a stile where the roofs of houses appear ahead. Follow the left-hand edge of a field and go over another stile onto a path between high hedges and trees. Go over a stile and continue between trees to join a short section of driveway by a house at Rosemerrin.

6 Turn right at a junction with the public road. Pass above the Maer Lake Nature Reserve. Continue to a junction and turn left into Maer Downs Road. In a few paces turn right to the car park.

🦋 ON THE WALK

Butterflies that are likely to be seen along the cliffs in summer include the meadow brown, the common blue and the colourful painted lady.

ROCKY BOUNDS OF BODMIN

A moorland walk across the exhilarating
wilds of Bodmin Moor.

Walk across London's Westminster Bridge and you walk across Bodmin Moor.
Granite used in the bridge comes from the now disused granite quarry of the
Cheesewring that dominates the eastern section of the moor near the village
of Minions. Bodmin Moor granite was also used in London's Albert Memorial
and in countless other structures worldwide, including a lighthouse in Sri
Lanka. Nineteenth-century stone workers extracted granite, not only from the
great raw gash of Cheesewring Quarry, but also from the wildest parts of the
moor such as the lower slopes of Kilmar Tor, on Twelve Men's Moor.

Cheesewring Quarry and Ancient Relics

Cheesewring Quarry is the torn-open heart of Stowe's Hill. It takes its name
from a remarkable granite 'tor', a pile of naturally formed rock that stands on
the quarry's lip. The name 'Cheesewring' comes from the tor's resemblance
to a traditional cider press, used to crush apples into a 'cheese'. There are
many similar 'cheesewrings' throughout Bodmin Moor, but none such as this.
Such formations were partly formed below ground millions of years ago,
and were then exposed when erosion sculpted the landscape. On the way
up to the Cheesewring, visit Daniel Gumb's Cave, a reconstructed version
of a rock 'house' once occupied by an 18th-century stone worker who was
also a self-taught philosopher and mathematician. On the roof you will see a
roughly carved theorem, though its authenticity is not proven. Beyond the
Cheesewring, the summit of Stowe's Hill is enclosed by an old 'pound', the
walls of a possible Bronze Age settlement.

Relics of a much older society than that of the quarry workers are found
at the start of the walk, where you pass the stone circles called The Hurlers.
These are remnants of Bronze Age ceremonial sites, though a later culture
created fanciful tales of the pillars, and those of the nearby 'Pipers'. Relish the
names, but reflect on the more intriguing Bronze Age realities. Beyond the
Cheesewring and The Hurlers, the walk will take you through a compelling
landscape, along the granite 'setts' or slabs of disused quarry tramways, and
past lonely tors at the heart of Bodmin Moor.

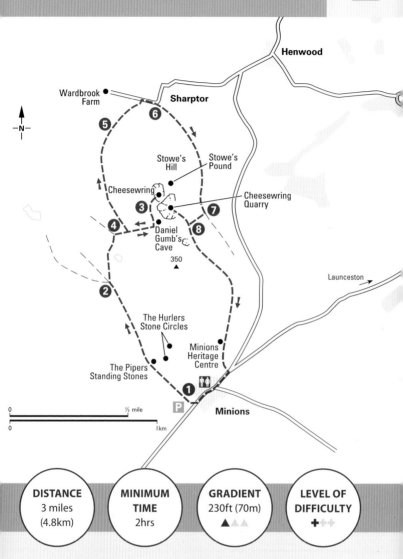

Henwood

Wardbrook Farm

Sharptor

⑥

⑤

−N−

Stowe's Hill

Stowe's Pound

Cheesewring

Cheesewring Quarry

③

⑦

④

⑧

Daniel Gumb's Cave

350 ▲

Launceston →

②

The Hurlers Stone Circles

Minions Heritage Centre

The Pipers Standing Stones

①

P

Minions

0 ½ mile

0 1km

DISTANCE
3 miles
(4.8km)

MINIMUM TIME
2hrs

GRADIENT
230ft (70m)
▲△△

LEVEL OF DIFFICULTY
✚✚✚

PATHS Moorland tracks and paths and disused quarry tramways

LANDSCAPE Open moorland punctuated with rocky tors

SUGGESTED MAP OS Explorer 109 Bodmin Moor

START/FINISH Grid reference: SX 260711

DOG FRIENDLINESS Keep under strict control around livestock

PARKING The Hurlers car park on south-west side of Minions village

PUBLIC TOILETS Minions village

WALK 2 DIRECTIONS

❶ Leave the car park by steps at its top end beside an information board about The Hurlers stone circles. Cross the grass to a broad stony track. Turn right and follow the track, passing The Hurlers circles on the right and the Pipers' stones further on.

❷ At a three-way junction, by a large granite block, take the right-hand track down through a shallow valley bottom, then climb uphill on a green track towards Cheesewring Quarry. At a junction with another track, cross over and follow a grassy track uphill towards the quarry. At the first green hillock, go sharp right, then round left to find Daniel Gumb's Cave. Return to the path and follow it uphill alongside the fenced-in rim of the quarry to the Cheesewring rock formation.

❸ Retrace your steps towards the shallow valley bottom.

❹ A short distance from the valley bottom, abreast of some thorn trees on the right and just before a fenced-off mound on the left, turn off right along a path. Keep to the left of the thorn trees and a big leaning block of granite and soon pick up the faint beginnings of a grassy track. Follow this track, keeping to the right of a thorn tree and gorse bushes. The track soon becomes much clearer.

❺ The track begins to strand. At a leaning rock, split like a whale's mouth, keep right along a path through scrub and with the rocky heights of Sharp Tor in line ahead. Keep to the path round the slope, with Wardbrook Farm left and Sharp Tor ahead. Reach a surfaced road and turn right for a few paces to reach an open gateway.

❻ Go to the right of the fence by the gateway and follow a path alongside the fence past two slim granite pillars. Join a disused tramway and follow this easy route.

❼ Pass some big piles of broken rock and, about 30yds (27m) beyond them, turn sharp right at a wall corner. Follow a green track uphill and alongside a wall. Where the wall ends keep on uphill to reach a broad track.

❽ Turn right along the track if you want to visit Cheesewring Quarry. For the main route, turn left and follow the track to Minions village. Pass the Minions Heritage Centre, a converted mine engine house. At the main road, turn right through the village to return to the car park.

> ### ⚘ IN THE AREA
> The natural resources of Bodmin Moor were exploited below ground as well as above. Its fascinating story is told at the Minions Heritage Centre in the refurbished Houseman's Engine House, once used to pump water from the South Phoenix Mine.

Opposite: Rock formations at Cheesewring Quarry

A KIT HILL CIRCUIT

A walk through a post-industrial landscape
that has been won back by nature.

Kit Hill was a busy industrial landscape during the 19th century but is now part of a World Heritage Site and lies within an Area of Outstanding Natural Beauty. The conical-shaped hill is over 1,000ft (305m) in height and dominates the countryside around the town of Callington. For today's visitor it offers a mix of typical moorland environment punctuated by the remnants of Victorian mining and quarrying.

Exotic Materials

Copper and tin were mined at Kit Hill for hundreds of years, but more exotic materials such as arsenic, fluorspar and wolfram were also found here. The old chimney stacks, pits, gullies and settling ponds of mineral extraction are now overgrown by a green pelt of grass and shrubby growth. The hacked and blasted walls of the old Kit Hill quarries are masked by trees and draped with plants and lichen. Scattered across the hill are the remains of a reputed 5,000 stone-splitting pits, many of them centuries old.

Prince Charles, the Duke of Cornwall, gave the hill and its surroundings to the people of Cornwall in 1985 to mark the birth of his eldest son, Prince William. In 2006 the hill became part of the Cornish Mining World Heritage Site and today, Kit Hill is managed as a country park by Cornwall Council.

Great Consols Mine

You start the walk from the summit of the hill, beside the mighty chimney stack of Kit Hill Great Consols mine, built in 1858. This complex was used for pumping water out of the mine and for lifting mineral ore to the surface. Later in the walk you pass the remains of South Kit Hill mine, dating from 1856. Look for the low circular stone mounds, known as buddles, which were used in separating tin from the crushed ore. It can be very busy around the hill's various car parks and the top car park especially is a favourite starting point for daily dog runs. Within minutes, however, you're likely to find yourself alone, strolling along pathways and tracks that lead to Kit Hill's sites of fascinating industrial archaeology amid havens of plant, insect and bird life.

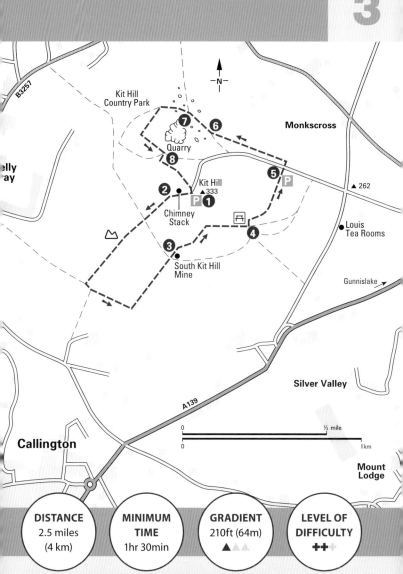

Kit Hill
Country Park

Monkscross

Kit Hill
▲333

Quarry

Chimney
Stack

▲ 262

Louis
Tea Rooms

South Kit Hill
Mine

Gunnislake →

Silver Valley

A139

Callington

½ mile

1km

Mount
Lodge

DISTANCE	MINIMUM TIME	GRADIENT	LEVEL OF DIFFICULTY
2.5 miles (4 km)	1hr 30min	210ft (64m) ▲▲▲	✚✚✚

PATHS Good throughout, but rocky in places **LANDSCAPE** A high isolated hill, typical of granite moorland; now a maintained country park **SUGGESTED MAP** OS Explorer 108 Lower Tamar Valley & Plymouth **START/FINISH** Grid reference: SX 375713 **DOG FRIENDLINESS** Dogs should be kept under control in areas where ponies may be grazing. They should also be kept on the lead during the bird-nesting season 1 March–31 July **PARKING** There are three car parks at Kit Hill. Use the car park at the summit of the hill **PUBLIC TOILETS** None on route **NOTE** The walk can be started from the Kit Hill middle car park at Point **5**

WALK 3 DIRECTIONS

❶ From the car park, go up a short path to the base of the mine chimney stack, then descend steps on its far side. Cross a flat grassy area, diagonally rightwards, to the beginning of a path beside a granite marker. Follow the path downhill, going through a wooden gate on the way.

❷ At the bottom of the slope, at a junction of paths, go left through a gate with a stile beside it. Continue along the path and, at a junction, go up the left-hand branch to the mine chimney stack of South Kit Hill mine.

❸ Keep to the left of the stack, pass an information panel and keep ahead, following a grassy track that winds round left and then uphill. At a junction bear right along the main track, passing to the left of a granite marker.

❹ Turn left through a wooden gate at the next junction. Go sharply right in front of a wooden bench and follow a sunken path between banks. Cross a wooden bridge over a ravine (note the eerie grid-covered mine opening down to the left) and soon reach the Kit Hill middle car park.

❺ Leave by the car park entrance, cross the road and go through a kissing gate. Follow a grassy track that soon becomes a rocky path. Beyond a bench, heaps of quarried granite appear ahead. Go through a kissing gate then a stand of dwarf oak.

> ### 🍴 EATING AND DRINKING
> Close to the entrance to Kit Hill is the Louis Tea Rooms where hot food and drinks, cakes and cream teas are available, with the bonus of terrific views down across the valley toward Plymouth Sound.

❻ Reach a T-junction with a track. Turn right and pass the entry to Kit Hill quarry. Keep straight ahead along a rocky path and bear left at a junction. Pass a huge iron ring bolt in a boulder and, in a few paces, take the left-hand path at another junction. Go through a wooden gate.

❼ Keep straight ahead up a rocky path. Keep left at a junction by a wooden post. Soon the summit chimney stack by the top car park comes into view.

> ### 🖈 IN THE AREA
> A visit to nearby Callington, with its attractive slate-hung houses, is worthwhile. There is a heritage centre in the town that has a great deal of information on the history of the Kit Hill area. It is open on Friday, Saturday, Sunday and Bank Holidays from mid-April to October.

❽ Go through a gate and turn left along a stony track. In about 80yds (73m) turn right along a grassy path between fenced off mine shafts and continue to the top car park.

TUDOR COTEHELE AND VICTORIAN CALSTOCK

A stroll along the River Tamar from Calstock's Victorian viaduct to the Tudor manor house of Cotehele.

A century ago Calstock was a bustling river port, and had been since Saxon times. Victorian copper and tin mining turned Calstock into an even busier port at which all manner of trades developed, including shipbuilding.

The coming of the railway brought an end to Calstock's importance. The mighty rail viaduct of 1906 that spans the river here is an enduring memorial to progress and to later decline, yet the Calstock of today retains the compact charm of its steep riverside location.

Cotehele

The area's finest architectural gem is the Tudor manor house of Cotehele, the focus of this walk. Cotehele dates mainly from the late 15th and early 16th centuries and the Edgcumbe family gave the house to the National Trust in 1947. Cotehele survives as one of the finest Tudor buildings in England. The medieval plan of the house is intact; the fascinating complex of rooms, unlit by artificial light, creates an authentic atmosphere that transcends any suggestion of 'theme park' history. This is a real insight into how wealthier people lived in Tudor Cornwall. Cotehele was built with privacy and even defence in mind and the materials used are splendidly rustic; the exterior façades have a rough patina that adds to the authenticity.

The Danescombe Valley

The early part of the walk leads beneath an arch of the Calstock Viaduct and on along the banks of the river, past residential properties where busy quays and shipbuilding yards once stood. Most of the walk leads through the deeply wooded Danescombe Valley, whose trees crowd round Cotehele in a seamless merging with the splendid estate gardens.

At Cotehele Quay, the preserved sailing barge, the *Shamrock*, and the National Maritime Museum's exhibition rooms, commemorate the great days of Tamar trade. As you walk back to Calstock, along an old carriageway and through Danescombe Valley, it is easy to imagine the remote, yet vibrant life of this once great estate and of the busy river that gave it substance.

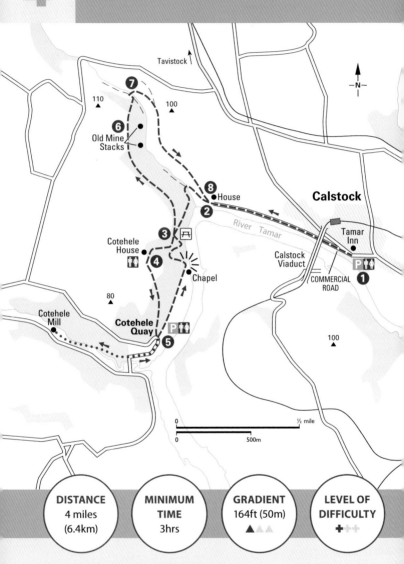

DISTANCE	MINIMUM TIME	GRADIENT	LEVEL OF DIFFICULTY
4 miles (6.4km)	3hrs	164ft (50m) ▲▲▲	✚✚✚

PATHS Excellent woodland tracks, can be muddy in places **LANDSCAPE** Wooded riverside **SUGGESTED MAP** OS Explorer 108 Lower Tamar Valley & Plymouth
START/FINISH Grid reference: SX 436685
DOG FRIENDLINESS Dogs should be kept under control in Cotehele environs
PARKING Calstock Quay car park. Bear right at junction at bottom of steep descent into village. Free car park, but limited spaces. Often full by mid-morning
PUBLIC TOILETS Calstock Quay, Cotehele House, Cotehele Quay

WALK 4 DIRECTIONS

❶ From the car park walk to the left of the Tamar Inn, then turn left into Commercial Road. In a few paces take the second turning left along Lower Kelly Lane and beneath Calstock Viaduct.

❷ Keep left at a fork just past the large house with a veranda. Beyond a row of cottages, branch left, signposted 'Cotehele House', and follow a broad track uphill and beneath trees.

❸ Go right at a junction, signposted 'Cotehele House'. Pass above a dovecote in Cotehele Gardens and then turn left at a T-junction. Go through a gate and turn right for the entrance to Cotehele House.

❹ Follow the road from Cotehele House, then branch left downhill to reach Cotehele Quay. (You can continue from the Quay for 0.5 miles/800m) to Cotehele Mill.)

❺ From the quay, follow a path that starts beside the car park and just beyond the Tamar Valley office. Pass a little chapel, then a superb viewpoint towards Calstock. At a junction, go right, signed to Calstock. In a few paces branch left to walk up a rising track.

❻ Go right at the second junction and descend to a wooden footbridge over a stream. At a T-junction with another track, turn left and walk up the track for about 55yds (50m).

❼ Turn sharply right and go up a rising track along the side of a stone wall. Pass a stone pillar and an old well on your left, then pass a junction with a track coming in from the left.

❽ Join the surfaced lane just before you reach the big house with a veranda, passed earlier. Retrace your steps to Calstock Quay.

ⓘ EATING AND DRINKING

The Barn Restaurant is an elegant National Trust eaterie within Cotehele House. It serves morning coffee, afternoon tea and meals using much local produce and has a fine wine list. The Edgcumbe Arms Tea Room on Cotehele Quay offers similar fare. The Tamar Inn at Calstock Quay is close to the start of the walk and is a traditional pub serving a range of bar meals.

🐾 ON THE WALK

The oak and beech woods that cloak the Danescombe Valley and Cotehele are a wildlife haven. The otter, an endangered species, may still be seen along the Tamar's banks. Buzzards lord it above clearings in the trees and along minor streams, kingfishers patrol their territory. In spring and early summer, the woods and meadows are thick with daffodils and bluebells.

A RAME HEAD RAMBLE

A rewarding walk round the Rame peninsula
offering peace and quiet within sight of Plymouth.

The Rame peninsula takes some getting to, but this delightful corner of
Cornwall offers rich rewards to the walker. You enjoy Cornwall in sight of
Devon's capital city and visit the village of Cawsand, once known for prolific
smuggling during the 18th and 19th centuries. Cawsand and Kingsand are
said to have handled over 17,000 casks of spirits in the one year of 1804 alone.
And this in full view of England's great navy in Plymouth Sound.

Grand Isolation

Such enterprise reflects Rame's grand isolation. The peninsula, together with
its neighbouring area of Maker and Mount Edgcumbe, is lodged in a corner
of Cornwall marked off by Plymouth Sound to the east and the estuary of
the River Lynher to the north. Roads wriggle their way onto the peninsula,
from the A38, dwindling in width as they unwind deeper into the area. For
centuries the Edgcumbe Estate shaped this remarkable coastal landscape
and on the route of your walk from Cawsand to the west, you follow the 'Earl's
Drive', built by an Earl of Mount Edgcumbe during the early 19th century.
Wealthy landowners of the time loved nothing more than transporting
impressionable guests in carriages about their grand 'picturesque' estates.

Historic Coastline

The walk leads along a historic coastline in more ways than one way. This was
an area of immense strategic importance to the defence of Britain throughout
the ages. Rame Head itself was used variously as an Iron Age 'fort', a lookout
and as the site of a signal beacon.

You can visit the summit of Rame Head and the ruin of the 14th-century
St Michael's chapel. On the west-facing coast of the headland you pass the
now privately owned Polhawn Fort, once part of a sequence of defences built
during the 1860s when fear of invasion from France was rife. The cost was
immense apparently and all to no avail. History apart, this walk entertains
with its wild flowers, its breathtaking sea views and the always busy offshore
traffic that sees everything from yachts to Naval destroyers passing by.

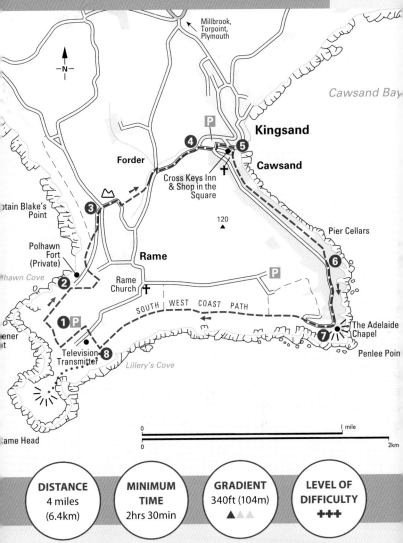

DISTANCE
4 miles
(6.4km)

MINIMUM TIME
2hrs 30min

GRADIENT
340ft (104m)
▲▲▲

LEVEL OF DIFFICULTY
+++

PATHS Occasionally muddy in winter on coast and field paths
LANDSCAPE Coastal area of low cliffs and headlands, wooded and
with open vegetated areas **SUGGESTED MAP** OS Explorer 108 Lower Tamar Valley
& Plymouth **START/FINISH** Grid reference: SX 421487
DOG FRIENDLINESS Ponies might be grazed on sections of the cliff tops from
November until May. Dogs should be kept on lead where notices indicate
PARKING Rame Head car park (adjacent to the National Coastwatch Institution
lookout) **PUBLIC TOILETS** Cawsand

WALK 5 DIRECTIONS

❶ Leave the car park through a kissing gate at the far corner nearest the Coastwatch lookout. Bear slightly right along a grassy track towards a wall and then follow the track gently downhill away from the wall to join the coast path and keep right. Cross a wooden footbridge and follow the coast path.

❷ Go through a kissing gate and follow the field-edge. Go through a kissing gate and follow a path between hedges. Keep left at a junction and descend steps. Cross a driveway and go down more steps. Turn right by a house and follow a driveway uphill. Turn left at a junction with another track and reach a junction of public roads.

❸ Keep straight across, ignoring the lane coming in from the right, and go down the main road opposite (with care) for about 120yds (110m). Just past a bend, go left through a kissing gate and follow the field-edge. Go through a kissing gate, turn right and, in a few paces, turn left along the main road.

❹ Turn right along a lane above a car park and just before a sign, 'Kingsand-Cawsand Twinned with Porspoder'. Soon, turn left down Armada Road, alongside the bottom edge of the car park, and follow the road round to reach The Square in Cawsand.

❺ Turn right, pass The Shop in The Square and, at a junction below the church, turn left along a lane, signed 'Coast Path'. This narrows to a surfaced path beyond two concrete posts. Cross a parking area beside houses and keep ahead through woods.

❻ Keep left at a junction with a surfaced lane. Go past a house and then bear right along a track past some lock-up garages. Soon, join a surfaced drive and go left. Emerge from the woods at Penlee Point above the Adelaide Chapel, which is reached down steps and a rocky path.

> ℗ **EATING AND DRINKING**
> In Cawsand's tiny Square is The Cross Keys Inn, which serves meals and pub lunches. Near by is the The Shop in the Square, which sells baguettes, baked potatoes and Cornish pasties as well as fish and chips.

❼ Continue along the coast path and, where the surfaced track swings abruptly right, keep straight ahead and through a kissing gate. Pass a signpost indicating a car park inland and soon pass another signpost to Rame Church. Keep to the coast path throughout.

❽ At a junction of tracks by a wooden bench (radio mast visible beyond the bench) turn right and follow a grassy track to a kissing gate into a lane and to the car park opposite. Alternatively you can keep ahead at the junction to visit the summit of Rame Head. This adds another 0.5 mile (800m) to the route.

THE DRAMATIC GEOLOGY OF CRACKINGTON HAVEN

A coastal and inland walk with views of the spectacular sea cliffs of the North Cornish coast.

Crackington Haven has given its name to a geological phenomena, the Crackington Formation, a fractured shale that has been shaped into incredibly twisted and contorted forms. On the sheared-off cliff faces of the area, you can see the great swirls and folds of this sedimentary rock that was transformed by volcanic heat and contorted by the geological storms of millions of years ago. Even the name Crackington derives from the Cornish word for sandstone, *crak*. The very sound of the word, in English, hints at a dangerous friability and dramatic decay. Scripted across the face of the vast cliffs traversed by this walk are the anticlines, (upward folds) and synclines (downward folds) that are so characteristic of these great earth movements.

Fantastic Rock

As you set out along the open cliff south from Crackington, the remarkable nature of the geology unfolds. Looking back on the coast path, you see clearly the massive contortions in the high cliff face of Pencannow Point on the north side of Crackington. Soon the path leads above Tremoutha Haven and up to the cliff edge beyond the domed headland of Cambeak. From here there is a breathtaking view of the folded strata and quartzite bands of Cambeak's cliffs. A path leads out to the tip of the headland, but it is precarious and is not recommended especially if it is wet or windy. The geology of the cliffs is still active, and, one day, erosion will destroy the neck of the headland, transforming Cambeak into an island, but preferably without you on it.

A short distance further on you arrive above Strangles Beach where again you look back to the Northern Door, a promontory of harder rock pierced by a natural arch where softer shales have been eroded by the sea. Where the route of the walk turns inland there is a line of low cliffs set back from the main cliff edge. These represent the old wounds of a land slip where the cliff has slumped towards the sea.

From here the second part of the walk turns inland and descends into East Wood and the peaceful Trevigue Valley and wandering down its leafy length is a splendid antidote to the coastal drama of the Crackington cliffs.

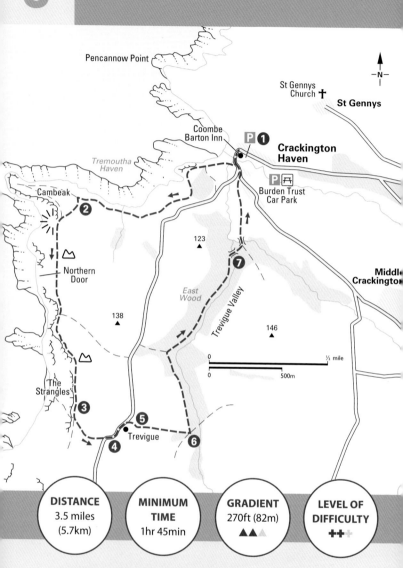

DISTANCE	MINIMUM TIME	GRADIENT	LEVEL OF DIFFICULTY
3.5 miles (5.7km)	1hr 45min	270ft (82m) ▲▲△	✚✚✚

PATHS Good coastal footpath and woodland tracks. Can be very wet and muddy **LANDSCAPE** Open coast and wooded valley
SUGGESTED MAP OS Explorer 111 Bude, Boscastle & Tintagel
START/FINISH Grid reference: SX 145969 **DOG FRIENDLINESS** Dogs on lead through grazed areas **PARKING** Crackington Haven car park. From the A39 at Wainhouse Corner, or from Boscastle on the B3263. Can be busy in summer. Burden Trust car park and picnic area **PUBLIC TOILETS** Crackington Haven

WALK 6 DIRECTIONS

1 From the Crackington Haven car park entrance go left across a bridge, then turn right at a telephone kiosk. Follow a broad track round to the left, between a signpost and an old wooden seat, then go through a kissing gate on to the coast path.

2 Eventually a stile leads to a steep stepped descent to footbridges below Cambeak and a path junction. Keep left and follow a path up a sheltered valley on the inland side of the steep hill, then continue on the cliff path.

3 At the start of a stretch of low inland cliff, pass a coast path post marked 'Trevigue'. Turn left at the next path to reach a road by a NT sign for 'Strangles'.

4 Go left, past the farm entrance to Trevigue, then, in a few paces, turn right down a drive by the Trevigue sign. Then bear off to the left across the grass to go through a gate with a yellow arrow.

5 Go directly down the field, keeping left of a telegraph pole, to reach a stile. Continue downhill to a stile on the edge of a wood. Continue down a tree-shaded path to a junction of paths in a shady dell by the river.

6 Turn sharp left here, following the signpost towards Haven, and continue on the obvious path down the wooded river valley.

7 Cross a footbridge, then turn left at a junction with a track. Cross another footbridge and continue to a gate by some houses. Follow a track and then a surfaced lane to the main road, then turn left to the car park.

❀ IN THE AREA
At Point **3**, where the route turns inland, you can continue along the coast path for a few paces to where a path leads down right to The Strangles beach, which is worth a visit, in spite of the steep return. You can view the remarkable coastal features from sea level.

☙ ON THE WALK
The field and woodland section of this walk supports a very different flora to that found on the heathery, windswept cliff land. Some of the most profuse field-edge and woodland plants belong to the carrot family, *Umbelliferae*. They may seem hard to distinguish, but the commonest is cow parsley, identifiable by its reddish stalk, feathery leaves and clustered white flower heads. Hogweed is a much larger umbellifer, often standing head and shoulders above surrounding plants; it has hairy stalks and broad-toothed leaves and can cause an unpleasant rash if it comes in contact with your skin. A third common umbellifer is the Alexander, prolific in spring and early summer. It has broad, lime green leaves and clustered yellow florets.

The unusual cliff geoglogy at Crackington Haven

THE SMUGGLERS' COAST AT TALLAND

A pleasant coastal walk through old-time smugglers' country.

If you love old churches that seem to grow from the very ground they stand on, then a visit to Talland church above Talland Bay near Polperro is a must. This is a wonderful building, part of which dates from the 13th century. Godliness seems to have gone hand in hand with rampant smuggling at Talland however. The area was a notorious smuggling centre in the 18th and 19th centuries.

Luxury Goods

The old smuggling days are long gone, of course, although modern smugglers attempted to land a drug consignment at Talland Bay during the 1980s but were foiled by the police and customs. Talland's old style smugglers dealt in a range of luxury goods, including the ubiquitous brandy, as well as fine cloth and even tea. The only people who were not involved in smuggling seem to have been the revenue men. Even an 18th-century vicar and noted exorcist, Richard Dodge, seems to have been up to his neck in the trade. Dodge encouraged stories of ghostly hauntings in the Talland Bay area to discourage people from travelling at night. He was even said to dress up in ghoulish costumes in which he leapt out on unsuspecting travellers who were innocently passing through the area, especially if a 'run ashore' by local smugglers was on hand.

High Point

Talland church is a high point of this walk. The church is built of local slate, a material that endows the building with a dark, mossy patina, which enhances its appeal even more. The tower of the church is three-storeyed and is detached from the main building although linked by a lovely porch with a wagon roof and weathered bosses. You'll see the village stocks inside the porch. The interior of the church is every bit as charming, not least the superb wagon roof in the south aisle and the carved bench ends. To the right of the door is a slate gravestone commemorating local man Robert Mark who is said to have been a popular smuggler and who was shot by the revenue men.

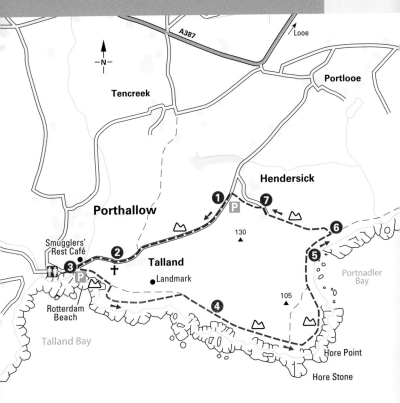

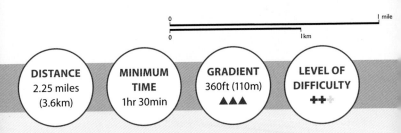

| DISTANCE 2.25 miles (3.6km) | MINIMUM TIME 1hr 30min | GRADIENT 360ft (110m) ▲▲▲ | LEVEL OF DIFFICULTY ✛✛+ |

PATHS Excellent throughout; can become muddy after prolonged rain; 1 stile

LANDSCAPE Gentle coastal area with occasional low cliffs

SUGGESTED MAP OS Explorer 107 St Austell & Liskeard

START/FINISH Grid reference: SX 236520

DOG FRIENDLINESS On lead in field areas

PARKING Hendersick National Trust car park

PUBLIC TOILETS 300yds (274m) west of Point ❸ on walk

WALK 7 DIRECTIONS

❶ Leave by the car park entrance and turn left along the surfaced lane. The lane descends quite steeply once over the brow of the hill. Watch out for traffic.

❷ Bear off left along a surfaced path to reach Talland church. On leaving the church turn right, through the porch exit and follow a grassy path through the graveyard to reach some steps. Go through a gate and rejoin the lane. Descend very steeply to reach Rotterdam beach, by the entrance to the Smugglers' Rest Café.

> **⏍ EATING AND DRINKING**
> The Smugglers' Rest Café is located in a lovely setting above the easterly beach of Talland Bay. They do breakfasts and offer a range of snacks including sandwiches, baguettes and salads as well as cream teas and ice cream and a range of hot and cold drinks.

❸ Turn sharp left and cross a small car park. Go through a gate and climb either of two sets of steep steps. Follow the coast path along the bottom edge of sloping fields. Dogs should be kept on lead here.

❹ Go through a kissing gate and continue along the coast path. Go up a series of steep steps and then cross a stile by a sign indicating the National Trust's Hendersick property.

> **⊘ IN THE AREA**
> Spend some time in Talland church's graveyard. This is not as ghoulish as it may seem. All graveyards are open books on the past and Talland has a remarkable number of dark slate gravestones, many of which relate, however briefly, thought-provoking stories of local families.

Continue along the coast path, going through a kissing gate and up a steep flight of steps on the way.

❺ Go through a kissing gate, cross a wooden bridge and then go through another kissing gate. Soon reach a gap between gorse bushes on your left, beside a wooden acorn coast path signpost.

❻ Turn left off the coast path and go uphill between the gorse bushes. Bear left along a slightly worn, but obvious path and then bear right and uphill to reach the outer corner of a wire fence. Continue walking up the path, with the fence on your right, to reach a gate. Go through the gate and continue along the path and then go through a gate with a barn to its left.

❼ Walk down a track for a few paces and then go left and follow a path through trees to another gate. Go through the gate, cross a track and go up a path to the car park.

BOSSINEY'S CLIFFS AND FAMOUS ROCKY VALLEY

Quiet field paths lead to a hike down
an atmospheric valley and along a dramatic coastline.

The village of Tintagel and its dramatic headland 'castle' is where Cornwall's King Arthur industry reaches a climax. It's a serious business for some, and good fun for all, but even King Arthur and all the trappings that go with him pale into insignificance before the truly awesome coastline of this part of North Cornwall. This lovely walk takes you from Tintagel's quieter neighbouring village of Bossiney through an inspiring landscape that needs no souvenirs to keep your memories fresh. You can even let your Arthurian imagination run riot as you walk down the atmospheric Rocky Valley.

Atmospheric Ruins

Rocky Valley is said to have been the last breeding ground of that other Arthurian symbol of ancient Cornwall, the red-legged, red-billed chough, a member of the crow family. The chough became extinct in the mid-20th century, although today it is being re-introduced in the far west of Cornwall. The stream that runs through Rocky Valley once supplied power to at least two mills. In the depth of the valley the footpath passes through the evocative ruins of Trewethet Mill where cloth and yarn were produced until 1861. What gives the site added interest are two labyrinth symbols, or petroglyphs, that are found on a natural rock wall among the ruins. As you descend to the buildings, first divert down to the right into an open area between the walls of the mill and a rock outcrop. Here on the smooth shale are carved two small labyrinth symbols that were uncovered from beneath lichen and vegetation in 1948 by a local man. They have since inspired much fanciful speculation to match the Arthurian excitement of Tintagel.

A large plaque on the rock wall above the carvings suggests a Bronze Age date for their creation but they are much more likely to have been the work of a reflective mill worker of the 18th or 19th centuries with time on their hands. From the Gothic depths of Rocky Valley, the walk takes you on to the high cliffs of Bossiney Common with impressive views of the vast cliffs and rocky pinnacles of Trewethet Gut and Saddle Rocks to the east and the great headland of Willapark to the west.

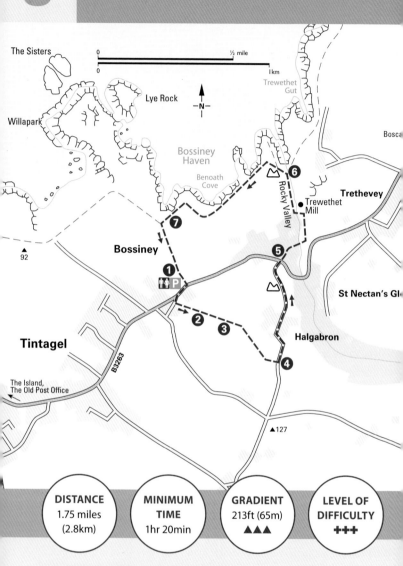

The Sisters

Lye Rock

Willapark

Bossiney
Haven

Benoath
Cove

Trewethet
Gut

Bosca

Trethevey

Rocky Valley

Trewethet
Mill

Bossiney

St Nectan's Gl

Tintagel

Halgabron

The Island,
The Old Post Office

B3263

▲92

▲127

0   ½ mile
0   1km

-N-

	DISTANCE	MINIMUM TIME	GRADIENT	LEVEL OF DIFFICULTY
	1.75 miles (2.8km)	1hr 20min	213ft (65m) ▲▲▲	+++

PATHS Easy field paths and rocky paths that can be awkward in places. All can be muddy underfoot during wet weather; 3 stiles **LANDSCAPE** A dramatic coastline of high cliffs and headlands backed by green fields and small wooded valleys **SUGGESTED MAP** OS Explorer 111 Bude, Boscastle & Tintagel **START/FINISH** Grid reference: SX 067889 **DOG FRIENDLINESS** Dogs on lead through fields and built-up areas **PARKING** Bossiney **PUBLIC TOILETS** Bossiney car park

WALK 8 DIRECTIONS

❶ Cross the main road from the car park, with care, then turn right past houses. In about 70yds (64m) turn left by the corner of a house, signposted 'Public Footpath'. Cross some gravel and then a grassy area and continue directly down a surfaced driveway with wooden holiday chalets on your left.

❷ Where the surfaced driveway bends round left, keep ahead, passing a final chalet on your left and go down a partially surfaced track. Just before the track peters out at a signpost to Halgabron, turn right and descend an awkward slate stile, or walk on a few paces and turn sharply round to the right. Cross a small bridge over a stream and go over a stile into a field.

🥾 ON THE WALK
Binoculars are useful on this walk. You may not spot a Cornish chough – give it time – but the coastal sections of this walk are the haunt of many seabirds, including puffins.

❸ Go up the steep field, bearing very slightly left, towards the opposite hedge. Go over a very high slate stile into a field. (The next section is a legally diverted right of way). Keep across the field, go over a stile and follow the right-hand edge of the next field. Go through a gate into a lane.

❹ Turn left and follow the narrow surfaced lane through the hamlet

🍴 EATING AND DRINKING
The best selection of places to eat is to be found in Tintagel. King Arthur's Arms Inn does meals and pub lunches and the Good Food Deli and Café offers ploughman's lunches, sandwiches and some fine real ales.

of Halgabron. Descend a final steep section to reach the main road.

❺ Cross the main road with great care and bear left down a surfaced driveway. Just before a house, go right, cross a wooden bridge and follow a rocky path alongside the often boisterous stream. Reach the ruins of Trewethet Mill where there are rock carvings. Cross a wooden bridge and continue to a junction with the coast path.

❻ Turn left along the coast path. (A rocky side path leads down right here towards some rock shelves. It can be dangerous when wet and is only for the agile.) Follow the coast path up steep steps. Bear round left where it levels off and follow the obvious well-worn path above the huge gulf of Benoath Cove and keep to the main path ahead.

❼ Descend steep, slate-faced steps into a deep trench above Bossiney Haven. You can descend to the beach here, but again this is only advised for the sure-footed and agile. Turn left and follow the path through fields towards a TV mast and the car park.

RIVERSIDE AND PEACEFUL FIELDS AT CAMELFORD

A reflective riverside walk leads to quiet lanes
and field paths through Camelford country.

Camelford nestles in the lush green valley of the River Camel on the western side of Bodmin Moor, a stone's throw from the rocky splendour of the high moorland hills of Rough Tor and Brown Willy. Yet in spite of this proximity to the moor, this undemanding walk enfolds you within a gentle and sheltered landscape of woods, fields and low hills drained by the infant river.

Royal Charter

The town of Camelford itself has a long and distinguished history. It originated as a strategic river crossing and was granted a Royal Charter as early as the 13th century, giving it the right to hold markets and fairs. The name Camelford has nothing to do with 'camels' in spite of the witty camel motif that embellishes the old Town Hall. The name is said to derive, rather prosaically, from the Cornish phrase for a bend in the river. The old coaching road to the west skirted the raw uplands of Bodmin Moor and passed through Camelford, ensuring the town's strategic importance. Today Camelford retains its strong historical character although it is partly robbed of inherent charm by incessant through-traffic.

Riverside Shade

A main road still squeezes through what is still, in terms of its narrow streets, the medieval heart of Camelford where a clutch of handsome buildings deserve a more peaceful setting. In spite of such close quarters' traffic, the start of this walk delivers you immediately into a world of riverside shade and quiet as you pass from Fore Street through an arched passageway called 'The Moors' onto the banks of the River Camel. Dappled shade and the tangled understorey of the trees create a pastoral mood that is a world away from the rugged heights of Bodmin Moor only a few miles to the east. The riverside path hops to and fro from bank to bank via worn old bridges and leads you downstream through green meadows. This pattern of deep countryside is sustained along a quiet lane to the farm hamlet of Treclago and on through sheltered fields that lead to another stream crossing and back to Camelford.

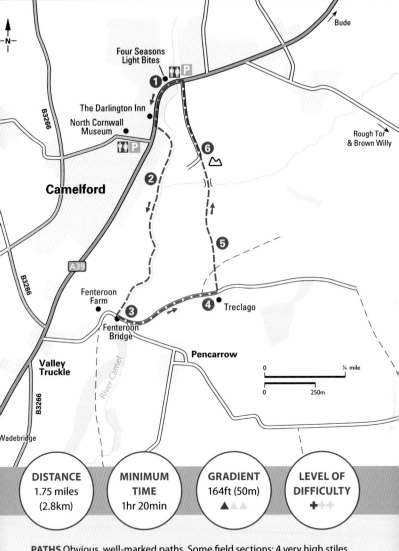

DISTANCE
1.75 miles
(2.8km)

MINIMUM TIME
1hr 20min

GRADIENT
164ft (50m)
▲▲▲

LEVEL OF DIFFICULTY
✚✚✚

PATHS Obvious, well-marked paths. Some field sections; 4 very high stiles
LANDSCAPE Wooded riverside, fields and quiet lanes **SUGGESTED MAP** OS
Explorer 109 Bodmin Moor **START/FINISH** Grid reference: SX 106838
DOG FRIENDLINESS Dogs on lead through grazed areas. Small dogs may find
high stiles difficult **PARKING** Car park at north entrance to Camelford, or small car
park opposite the North Cornwall Museum **PUBLIC TOILETS** Near main car park
by the entrance to Enfield Park. At car park opposite North Cornwall Museum

WALK 9 DIRECTIONS

❶ Cross from the main car park and turn right along Fore Street until about 50yds (46m) beyond The Darlington Inn. Go left through an archway, signed 'To the River and Advent Church'. (This point can be reached from the car park opposite North Cornwall Museum by walking down to the main road and turning left.) Follow the riverside path downstream.

❷ Cross a bridge to the left bank. Cross back to the right bank on a narrow bridge that has no guard rail on its downstream side. Continue walking past a waste water treatment works and follow the path through some meadows.

❸ Go up a slate step stile into a surfaced lane and turn left across Fenteroon Bridge. Keep left immediately at a junction and follow a narrow lane uphill between low walls that are covered in moss and ivy.

❹ At Treclago keep to the right of the first buildings and then turn sharply left opposite some barns and go up a track. Keep straight on across a track

junction, go through a wooden gate and follow the track ahead. This section can be extremely muddy and mucky from cattle but soon becomes stonier.

❺ Go through a metal gate into a field and keep straight ahead and downhill. Go through a small metal gate and over a wooden stile and then cross a narrow bridge with step-over bars at either end. Go steeply uphill and over a very high slate stile. Follow a grassy path to a high stile into a lane by houses.

❻ Keep straight ahead along College Road to reach Camelford and the car park opposite.

---

❷ IN THE AREA

Have a look at Camelford's Market Place and its historic buildings such as the Town Hall with its golden camel weather vane and fine leaded glass window, again with a camel motif. The handsome Warmington House opposite has unusual wooden window lintels. From Market Place walk along Chapel Street with its cobbled rainwater gullies and be sure to visit the excellent North Cornwall Museum in Clease Road.

❨❩ EATING AND DRINKING

Camelford has many food outlets. There are a number of cafés and restaurants including the pleasant Four Seasons Light Bites, just across from the main car park. They offer drinks and snacks, freshly baked Cornish pasties and cream teas. Dogs are welcomed. Local pubs, The Masons' Arms and The Darlington Inn both do bar meals.

BY WOODS AND WATER AT CARDINHAM

A riverside woodland walk that passes the ghostly ruins of an abandoned lead and silver mine.

Forget the Cornish sea for once on a walk that takes you into the heart of inland Cornwall at the green and peaceful world of Cardinham Woods near Bodmin. This vast swathe of woodland supports a traditional mix of ancient oaks, beech, hazel and holly alongside commercial conifers. The first and last sections of the walk are level and well suited to children's buggies with sturdy and stable wheels. You can miss out the steep and rougher middle section to the Wheal Glynn Mine if you want to take very young children for a spin.

Lush Countryside

Cardinham Woods lies to the east of Bodmin town in lush countryside drained by the Cardinham Water and its tributaries. The 650 acres (263ha) that make up Cardinham have been in the hands of the Forestry Commission since 1922 and still were at the time of writing but have since been put up for sale by the government. The original woodland was used for such traditional rural industries as charcoal burning and coppicing. Most of the tracks and paths through the woods are courtesy of the woodland management and you should check any notices indicating where work is being carried out.

Clapper Bridge

Just below the modern forestry bridge and beside an old ford is a 'clapper' bridge that crosses the stream. Now blocked off for safety reasons, this was known as Lady Vale Bridge and was a major crossing point for many years.

Somewhere within the tangle of woodland behind the bridge is the site of Lady Vale Chapel, an early Christian site. From Lady Vale you can head back downriver for an easier return to the car park. Otherwise the main walk climbs high into Hurtstocks Wood, a witch-world of dense trees whose moss-covered trunks are entwined with thick columns of ivy that may send a shiver up your spine. At the highest point of the route the towering chimneystack of the old Wheal Glynn silver mine suddenly looms into view. Its dark slatey stonework is so swathed in gnarled ivy branches that it looks like a mighty tree trunk in its own right.

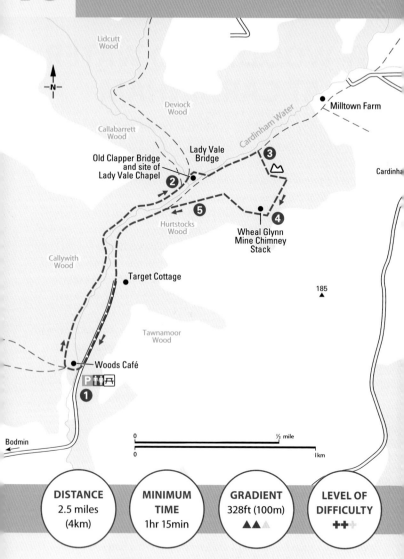

WALK 10 DIRECTIONS

❶ From the car park, cross the wooden bridge over Cardinham Water and pass through the café and play area. Bear left, then right and then round right to go through a wooden barrier to reach a three-way junction. Keep straight ahead and follow a broad forestry track with the Cardinham Water down to your right. Ignore all side tracks.

❷ Pass a junction with a track on the left and cross a bridge. Keep round to the right, ignoring junctions left, and cross Lady Vale Bridge. Turn left at a junction with a broad track, signposted 'Wheal Glynn'. (For an easy return, especially for pushchairs, turn right and follow the track back to the car park.)

🐾 ON THE WALK

If you are very lucky – and very quiet – you may spot the elusive roe deer among the deeper woodland. This is a small, handsome little deer with a red-brown summer coat and long grey winter coat. The small antlers are very upright and usually have only three points.

---

❸ Where the track widens, in about 0.25 miles (400m), turn sharply right, signposted 'Wheal Glynn', and follow a rough track steeply uphill. Keep straight ahead at a junction. Keep round left and uphill at a fork beside a wooden bench to reach a junction with a broad track by a wooden railing.

❹ Turn right and soon pass the stack of Wheal Glynn mine. Follow the track round right and over a bridge. Soon reach a junction with a wide track by a wooden bench. Keep right and ahead.

❺ Descend along the wide track. Keep left at the junction with the track from Lady Vale Bridge. Follow the track with the river below, pass two houses and keep on to return to the car park.

🔎 IN THE AREA

St Meubred's Church at Cardinham village a few miles to the north east of Cardinham Woods' car park is a handsome building. The churchyard boasts two of the finest ancient crosses in Cornwall. The aisles of the church have fine wagon roofs, some of which retain their original colouring, and are matched for style by 15th to 16th-century bench ends.

🍴 EATING AND DRINKING

Beside the Cardinham Woods car park there is a delightful riverside café called Woods, located in an old cottage. It serves morning coffee, lunches and afternoon tea. There is a wide range of food outlets in Bodmin, 4 miles (6.4km) away, but if you want an authentic country pub try the London Inn at St Neot, 8 miles (12.9km) to the east of Cardinham Woods.

THROUGH THE DEEP HEART OF CORNWALL

An easy ramble along the peaceful Lerryn Creek and on through Ethy Wood.

There are corners of Cornwall that seem so well hidden that you begin to suspect that they may move around at night just to catch you out. The village of Lerryn, between the town of Lostwithiel and the port of Fowey, is one such place. It is worth finding all the same.

Lerryn is far from being 'landlocked' in fact. It was once a seagoing port for sailing barges that crept upriver via the River Fowey to the tidal headwaters of the tributary River Lerryn. They carried limestone and coal for the kilns that stood near the village and which produced lime for fertilising local fields. The barges also fetched and carried goods to and from the old Ethy Estate that lay at Lerryn and from the village and surrounding farms. The deep woods of the area produced charcoal, pit props and bark that would have been shipped downriver to seagoing vessels moored at Fowey. This was the Cornwall of waterborne transport, when even such a lovely lost backwater as Lerryn was linked to the great outside world by water rather than by rough tracks and turnpike roads. Today, Lerryn Creek is deeply silted, although small leisure boats still use river and creek when high tide draws a shining sleeve of water over the mousse-like mud banks.

Ancient Oaks

The walk you follow curls its way along the bank of Lerryn Creek and then climbs inland through Ethy Wood, once part of the Ethy Estate and now in the care of the National Trust. This is a green world of ancient oak trees and other mixed woodland that shelters a perennially damp understorey where mosses, ferns and woodland plants grow in profusion. Ethy Wood has been identified as a nationally important area for lichens. The creek and its wooded banks also have a fascinating claim to literary fame being said to have inspired Kenneth Grahame's *Wind in the Willows* (1908). Grahame often stayed at Fowey and made boat trips upriver to Lerryn and it's not too fanciful to imagine him basing Rat and Mole's river picnic on Lerryn's perfect river setting. Lerryn village still retains such timeless charm. At low water, stepping stones span the river. They are fit to cross – at your own risk, of course.

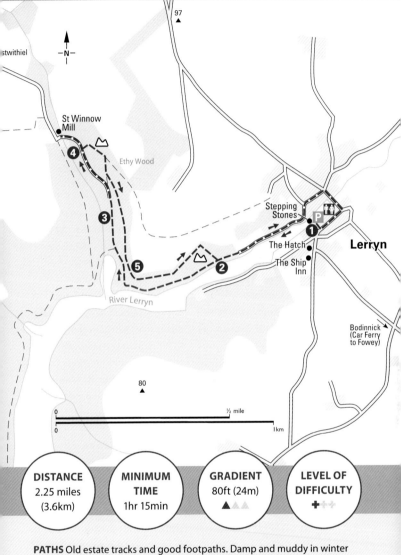

DISTANCE	MINIMUM TIME	GRADIENT	LEVEL OF DIFFICULTY
2.25 miles (3.6km)	1hr 15min	80ft (24m) ▲▲▲	✚✚✚

PATHS Old estate tracks and good footpaths. Damp and muddy in winter
LANDSCAPE Wooded headwaters of the tidal River Lerryn with mudbanks
at low tide **SUGGESTED MAP** OS Explorer 107 St Austell & Liskeard
START/FINISH Grid reference: SX 140570
DOG FRIENDLINESS Good. But keep within reasonable control near
fields and houses **PARKING** Lerryn car park
PUBLIC TOILETS Next to Lerryn Memorial Hall

WALK 11 DIRECTIONS

❶ Cross the river from the car park by the stepping stones, if feasible and at your own risk. Alternatively, turn left out of the car park pass the Lerryn Memorial Hall and follow the road round left and across the river bridge. Take the first turning left and, at a T-junction, go left to the riverside opposite the car park. Turn right along a river bank lane.

❷ Go along a track into the woods, beyond the last house. Pass a stone pillar and bear round right to reach the banks of a small inlet at Ethy Quay. Continue along the track and, where the path forks at the head of the inlet, take the right-hand branch over a rocky section at first.

> ### ⚓ ON THE WALK
> Ethy Wood is the ideal environment for such plants as hart's tongue fern with its long spade-like leaves and polypody fern, a small-leaved glossy fern that grows on tree trunks. You may well spot a heron on the creek banks, as well as waders such as curlew and dunlin. Even a dedicated seagoer like the cormorant sometimes wings its way this far inland.

> ### 🍴 EATING AND DRINKING
> The name of The Ship Inn at Lerryn says everything about the area's historic seagoing connections. They serve pub lunches here. Just by the car park entrance is The Hatch, adjoining the Lerryn River Stores. The Hatch offers snacks, food platters and hot drinks. There are useful picnic tables by the river.

❸ Reach another junction then take the left-hand branch. Pass above a house, once St Nott's Mill, and continue along the main track.

❹ Reach a junction with a path going off right. (You can continue on the main path for a short distance to the derelict St Winnow Mill and then return to the junction.) Turn right along this path into the woods. Keep right at a junction, and then keep left at the next junction.

❺ Just past a field gate, the track becomes a narrow path. Follow this path through tall pine trees and quite steeply downhill to re-join the creekside track used on the outgoing section of the walk. Turn left and return to Lerryn and the car park.

> ### 🌐 IN THE AREA
> If you have time you can extend your walk by 2 miles (3.2km), from just past St Winnow Mill, by turning left at a junction and continuing to St Winnow Church. From here a path leads along the banks of the River Fowey to St Winnow Point and then turns north alongside Lerryn Creek to the inlet at Ethy Rock.

A GLIMPSE OF OLD CORNWALL AT POLRUAN

A woodland and coastal walk from the village of Polruan
through the ancient parish of Lanteglos.

The green headland on which Polruan stands has the sea on its southern
shore and is bounded to the north by the calm and tree-lined tidal creek of
Pont Pill. The village can be reached by land only along fairly minor roads that
detour at some length from Cornwall's main spinal highways. Yet Polruan lies
across the estuary from the bustling town of Fowey and a regular passenger
ferry runs between the two.

Old Cornwall
Prehistoric settlers found a natural refuge on this narrow headland. Christian
'saints' and medieval worshippers set up chantries and chapels in the
sheltered hollows; merchants prospered from the sea trade into Fowey's
natural harbour. During the wars of the 14th and 15th centuries, Fowey
ships harried foreign vessels, and because of their outstanding seamanship,
earned themselves the sobriquet of 'Fowey Gallants'. The entrance to the
estuary was protected from attack by a chain barrier that could be winched
across the river's mouth from blockhouses on either bank. In peacetime the
Gallants continued to raid shipping of all types until Edward IV responded to
complaints from foreign merchants, and several English ones, by confiscating
ships and by having the protective chain removed. Resilient as always, the
seamen of Fowey and Polruan turned their hands to fishing and smuggling.

From Polruan, the walk wanders through countryside that was once owned
by wealthy medieval families who played a major part in organising the
freebooting activities of Polruan seamen. Original fortunes made through
piracy were turned to legitimate trade and to farming and land management,
and the countryside through which the walk leads is the product of long-term
land ownership and rural trade. At its heart lies the splendid Lanteglos Church
of St Winwaloe, or St Willow. The second part of the walk leads back to the
sea, to the steep headland of Pencarrow and to the dramatic amphitheatre of
Lantic Bay with its fine beach, an old smugglers domain if ever there was one.
From here, the coastal footpath leads back to Polruan and to the rattle and
hum of an estuary that has never ceased to be alive with seagoing vessels.

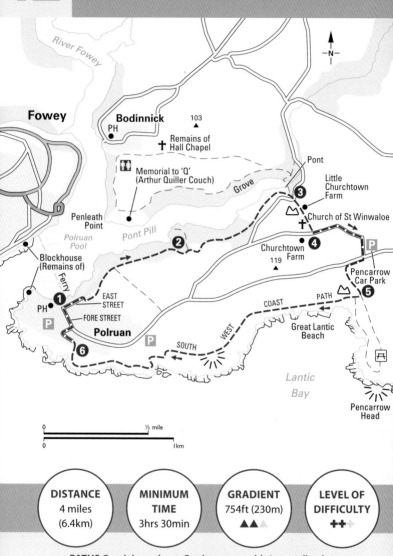

DISTANCE	MINIMUM TIME	GRADIENT	LEVEL OF DIFFICULTY
4 miles (6.4km)	3hrs 30min	754ft (230m) ▲▲▲	++✛

PATHS Good throughout. Can be very muddy in woodland areas during wet weather **LANDSCAPE** Deep woodland alongside tidal creek. Open coastal cliffs **SUGGESTED MAP** OS Explorer 107 St Austell & Liskeard **START/FINISH** Grid reference: SX 126511 **DOG FRIENDLINESS** Dogs on lead through grazed areas. Notices indicate **PARKING** Polruan. An alternative start to the walk can be made from the National Trust Pencarrow car park (Point ❹ SX 149513). You can also park at Fowey's Central car park, then catch the ferry to Polruan **PUBLIC TOILETS** Polruan

WALK 12 DIRECTIONS

❶ Walk up from the Quay at Polruan, then turn left along East Street, by a telephone box and a seat. Go right, up steps, signposted 'To the Hills' and 'Hall Walk'. Go left at the next junction, then keep along the path ahead. Keep right at a junction and pass a National Trust sign, 'North Downs'.

❷ Turn right at a T-junction with a track, then in just a few paces, bear off left along a path, signposted 'Pont and Bodinnick'. Reach a wooden gate on to a lane. Don't go through the gate, but instead bear left and go through a footgate. Follow a path, established by the National Trust, and eventually descend steep wooden steps.

❸ At a T-junction with a track, turn right and climb uphill. It's worth diverting left at the T-junction to visit Pont. On this route, reach a lane. Go left for a few paces then, on a bend by Little Churchtown Farm, bear off right through a gate signed 'Footpath to Church'. Climb steadily to reach the Church of St Winwaloe.

🏤 EATING AND DRINKING

There are no refreshment opportunities on the walk, but the Russell Inn at the bottom of Fore Street, Polruan and the Lugger Inn on Polruan Quay, both do good pub lunches. There are a number of cafés and restaurants in Polruan. The Old Ferry Inn at Bodinnick also does pub lunches.

---

❹ Turn left outside the church and follow a narrow lane. At a T-junction, just beyond Pencarrow car park, cross the road and go through a gate, then turn right along the field-edge on a path established by the National Trust, to go through another gate. Turn left along the field-edge.

❺ At the field corner, turn right on to the coast path and descend very steeply. (To continue to Pencarrow Head go left over the stile and follow the path on to the headland. From here the coast path can be rejoined and access made to Great Lantic Beach.) Follow the coast path for about 1.25 miles (2km), keeping to the cliff edge ignoring any junctions.

❻ Where the cliff path ends, go through a gate to a road junction. Cross the road then go down School Lane. Turn right at 'Speakers Corner', then turn left down Fore Street to reach the Quay at Polruan.

🍂 ON THE WALK

Spend some time exploring Polruan, at the beginning or end of the walk. This fine little port has retained much of its vernacular character in spite of some modern development. Polruan thrived because of seagoing and there is still a rich sense of those former sea-dominated days in the narrow alleyways of the village.

View across the Fowey River to Polruan

A RAMBLE AROUND THE RUMPS

A breezy walk round the National Trust headland of The Rumps.

In Cornwall you are spoiled for choice when it comes to mighty headlands above the glittering sea. This walk takes you onto one of the mightiest, at Pentire on the northern arm of Padstow Bay, the great estuary of the River Camel. The headland is ringed by towering black cliffs that rise to over 300ft (91m) in height, the remnants of volcanic upheavals of millions of years ago.

Dramatic Pinnacles

Pentire's most northerly point is dominated by the twin-lobed promontory of The Rumps, a rugged and sea-battered fist of land embellished with dramatic pinnacles and with an accompanying offshore island known as The Mouls. The shape of The Rumps, a projecting promontory linked to the main headland by a neck of land, makes it clear why this was once the site of an Iron Age 'cliff castle' or 'promontory fort'. The corrugated folds of three earth ramparts, with accompanying ditches, lie across the narrowest part of the neck and extend down either side to the very edge of the cliffs. The outermost rampart has a stone flanked entrance 'gateway'. This would have been closed off with a massive wooden gate when the site was occupied during the period from about the 2nd century BC until the 1st century AD. Excavations were carried out here during the 1970s and late Iron Age pottery was found. There are also traces of Iron Age round houses at the site.

Cliff Castle

Early interpretations of these ancient sites explained them as being entirely defensive, hence the 'cliff castle' label. The obvious defensive potential of the ramparts certainly seems to indicate this. Later thinking, however, suggests that such promontory sites might simply have been commercial and cultural centres where local Iron Age communities and visiting merchants met. Here they would trade, exchange news and negotiate over the territorial and civil issues that were emerging as a more settled society put down deeper roots. The ramparts might simply have served to distinguish the sites as being of major economic, social and cultural importance.

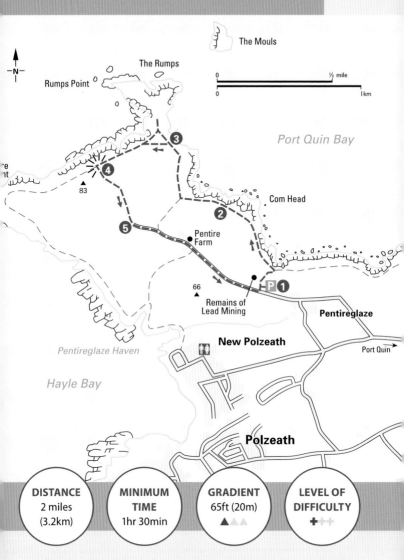

The Mouls

The Rumps

Rumps Point

—N—

Port Quin Bay

③

④

83

②

Com Head

⑤

Pentire Farm

66

Remains of Lead Mining

Pentireglaze

P ①

New Polzeath

Port Quin

Pentireglaze Haven

Hayle Bay

Polzeath

0 ½ mile
0 1 km

DISTANCE	MINIMUM TIME	GRADIENT	LEVEL OF DIFFICULTY
2 miles (3.2km)	1hr 30min	65ft (20m) ▲▲▲	✦✦✦

PATHS Clearly identifiable and good underfoot. Paths can be wet and muddy after heavy rain and are usually so in winter; 1 stile **LANDSCAPE** A rugged flat-topped headland of very high cliffs backed by typical coastal heathland and close-cropped grass **SUGGESTED MAP** OS Explorer 106 Newquay & Padstow **START/FINISH** Grid reference: SW 940799 **DOG FRIENDLINESS** Under control in areas where sheep or ponies might be grazed **PARKING** National Trust car park just beyond Pentireglaze **PUBLIC TOILETS** New Polzeath

WALK 13 DIRECTIONS

❶ From the top corner of the car park take the footpath beside the National Trust map and information board. Soon cross a field and go through a gate to join the coastal footpath, signposted 'The Rumps'. Turn left along the coast path.

❷ Go through a gate (dogs on lead here). Go up steps and on down the slope and through another gate, continuing along the cliff edge. Go through another gate and reach a junction.

❸ Take the right-hand branch to visit the protruding headland of The Rumps proper. Returning from The Rumps take the right-hand path and rejoin the coast path.

🍴 **EATING AND DRINKING**

The Doom Bar of the Atlantic House Hotel, Little Polzeath does breakfasts, bar food and evening meals. You can enjoy a range of tasty sandwiches, hot dogs or salads among many other choices.

❹ Turn off left from the coast path at a signpost to Pentire Farm. Go through a gate and follow the left edge of the next two fields.

❺ Go over a wooden stile next to a wooden gate and into a stony lane. Walk along the lane towards Pentire Farm and continue along the track to return to the car park.

🥾 **ON THE WALK**

As always on such coastal headlands the environment seems entirely natural. Yet beside the car park you may notice several low hummocks. These are the surviving elements of an old lead mine that operated at various times from as early as the 16th century until late Victorian times.

🌐 **IN THE AREA**

A mile (1.6km) or so to the east, along the coast road, lies the tiny hamlet of Port Quin. There is a haunting atmosphere about Port Quin today. This was a busy settlement in previous centuries when fishing boats and trading vessels anchored in the sheltered inlet. Until the mid-19th century up to 100 people lived at Port Quin. The dramatic depopulation has been explained as perhaps being caused by a disaster at sea in which the men of the cove were lost, although the economic decline of fishing and mining is the more likely reason.

TREVONE AND GUNVER HEAD

A view of Gunver Head's eye-catching cliffs
and of a very big hole in the ground.

Go for a walk at Gunver Head and you see spectacular geology at every turn.
Cornwall is at the cutting edge of coastal geology in more ways than one. The
county's coastline is where erosion by sea and weather and by simple gravity
holds sway. Together these forces of nature have exposed the geological lie
of the land to show us what the ground beneath our feet is made of.

Golden Sand and Chess Pieces
The walk starts at Trevone Bay, where land and sea meet gently at a broad
apron of tide-washed golden sand. From the beach at Trevone the walk leads
inland along lanes and farm tracks past the hamlet of Crugmeer. Beyond here
the coast is reached at Gunver Head where the serious geology begins. Giant
pinnacles and tottering lumps of rock are made up of masses of shale shot
through with myriad complexities – the end products of cataclysmic earth
movements millions of years ago. What we see, in fact, are the wasted and
eroded roots of mountains that were formed during vast earth movements,

These fantastic giant chess pieces are easily viewed from the cliff path. The
Meropes are a sequence of offshore islands and rocky stacks that lie a mere
stone's throw from the mainland beyond a narrow rocky channel known
as Tregudda Gorge. The most distinctive of the stacks is Middle Merope, a
slender offshore tower of earth and rock that culminates in a narrow flat-
topped pinnacle. Further south from The Meropes is the feature known as
Porthmissen Bridge, a huge grass-topped bulwark, which is linked to the
mainland by a very narrow ridge of rock, earth and grass and is pierced by
an archway at sea level. Further south again is the Marble Cliff on which over
140 parallel bands of shale and limestone create a fascinating pattern. The
area's remarkable geology is not finished yet. Keep to the cliff edge path
that leads back towards Trevone and you reach Round Hole Point, a sunny
little headland of tan-coloured dolerite rock. Just a few paces inland from
the point is the spectacular Round Hole, a huge circular pit, over 80ft (24m)
deep caused by the sea effectively tunnelling into the base of the cliff and
undermining the soft ground above until it collapsed.

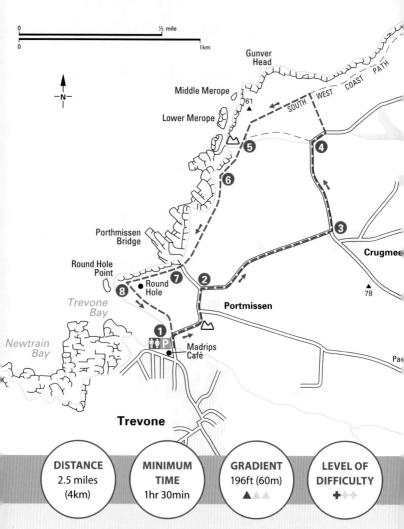

½ mile

1km

Gunver Head

Middle Merope

Lower Merope

61

SOUTH WEST COAST PATH

5

4

6

Porthmissen Bridge

3

Crugmee

Round Hole Point

7

2

78

8

Round Hole

Portmissen

Trevone Bay

Newtrain Bay

1

Madrips Café

Pa

Trevone

DISTANCE	MINIMUM TIME	GRADIENT	LEVEL OF DIFFICULTY
2.5 miles (4km)	1hr 30min	196ft (60m) ▲▲▲	✦✦✦

PATHS Farm tracks and easy clifftop paths. Take care near cliff edges; 4 stiles

LANDSCAPE A coastline of fascinating rock formations and unique geology

SUGGESTED MAP OS Explorer 106 Newquay & Padstow

START/FINISH Grid reference: SW 892759

DOG FRIENDLINESS Dogs should be kept under control in field sections and on open cliff where cattle may be grazing

PARKING Trevone Beach **PUBLIC TOILETS** Trevone car park

WALK 14 DIRECTIONS

❶ Go down steps at the café end of the car park and to the left of the café entrance. Turn left and follow a lane that bends right above the beach. Keep to this lane as it rises uphill.

❷ Stay on the lane where it levels off at a junction with a track to the left. Go through a gapway and continue along the surfaced lane through open fields to the little hamlet of Crugmeer.

❸ Turn left at Crugmeer and follow a narrow lane towards the coast. Follow the road round to the right past a small parking area.

❹ Pass another small parking area in about 30yds (27m) and in a few paces go left down a short-lived overgrown path and cross a wooden stile into a field. Follow the right-hand edge of the field to reach a junction with the coast path. Turn left and follow the coast path round Gunver Head.

❺ Follow the path steeply downhill into the bottom of a narrow valley and continue less steeply uphill to

reach a high slate stile. Cross a wooden footbridge and continue uphill to where the path levels off. There are dramatic views back to Lower Merope Island and Middle Merope.

❻ Continue along the coast path and cross another high stile. Beyond here, either stay close to the cliff edge or follow a broad grassy track well inland from the cliff edge. Reach a gravelly track and several paces ahead bear off right along a grassy path. Skirt round some ruined walls. Porthmissen Bridge is visible to the right.

❼ Keep to the right and follow the coast path to the rocky headland of Round Hole Point where there are picnic spots below the path. Just inland from the Point is the famous Round Hole. Take great care if looking down from the edges of the hole.

❽ Continue along the coast path. Cross a stone stile and reach concrete steps that lead down to the lane at Trevone Beach. Turn right, cross above the beach and return to the car park.

A MEANDER DOWN THE MEVAGISSEY COAST

A walk to a beautiful low-lying
headland close to the sea.

An authentic flavour of Old Cornwall clings firmly to the fishing port of Mevagissey, or 'Meva' to locals, in spite of the village's popularity in summer. There has been some unsympathetic development in Mevagissey but the older part of the port retains a rich vernacular character in its colourwashed buildings and narrow streets and its inner and outer harbours.

The walk starts at the tiny settlement of Portmellon, where sturdy Cornish fishing boats, yachts and launches were once built at the Percy Mitchell boatyard. The slipway on the seaward side of the road survives and when vessels, many of them over 50ft (15m) in length, were ready for launching, they were towed from the boatyard on a trolley, across the road and then launched from the slipway. Just beyond the slipway, your route veers off along the route of the coast path and on to the delightful twin headlands of Chapel Point and Turbot Point, with Colona Beach between. Chapel Point is a low-lying section of coast where the closer merging of sea with land imparts a wonderful sense of freshness and open space. The handsome dwellings on the point were built in the 1930s. They are in the Neo-Rustic style, which uses such features as turrets, steeply pitched roofs, tall chimneys and tall narrow windows to create an impression of almost monastic architecture.

Bodrugan's Leap

Between Chapel Point and Turbot Point is the lovely Colona Beach. Turbot Point has the alternative name of Bodrugan's Leap. The name derives from an apocryphal event during which local landowner and 15th-century worthy, Sir Henry Trenowth of nearby Bodrugan is said to have leapt from his horse into a waiting boat while being pursued by Sir Richard Edgcumbe of Cothele. Sir Richard had been ordered by the authorities to arrest Bodrugan, who for years had slipped easily between legitimate business and piracy. Off to France went Bodrugan and his lands were confiscated, no doubt to the benefit of Edgcumbe and the ruling interests of the day. From this romantic reference point you turn inland alongside a tiny stream to the public road and a steep descent to Portmellon and perhaps on to Meva for an additional treat.

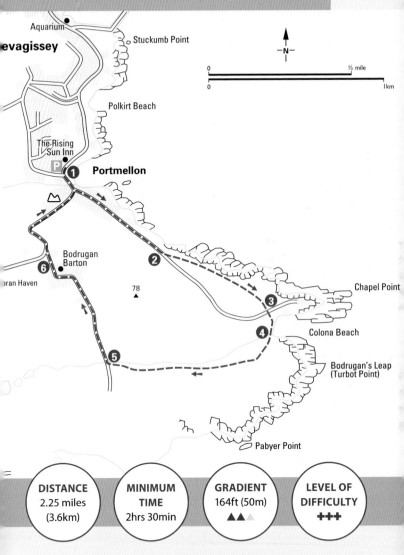

DISTANCE
2.25 miles
(3.6km)

MINIMUM TIME
2hrs 30min

GRADIENT
164ft (50m)
▲▲▲

LEVEL OF DIFFICULTY
+++

PATHS Excellent throughout, but can be very muddy in wet conditions; 2 stiles
LANDSCAPE A low coastline and rocky foreshore with the land rising steeply
behind **SUGGESTED MAP** OS Explorer 105 Falmouth & Mevagissey
START/FINISH Grid reference: SX 016439 **DOG FRIENDLINESS** Dogs on lead
through fields and by houses **PARKING** Car park of The Rising Sun Inn (pay
parking fee in pub; car park closed January and February) or streetside where
legitimate and without obstructing traffic **PUBLIC TOILETS** None on route

WALK 15 DIRECTIONS

❶ Leave the car park at Portmellon and walk south along the seafront road. Walk uphill for 25yds (23m) and then turn off left, signposted 'Coast Path'. Continue along a surfaced road.

❷ Just before a small stand of trees, turn left from the surfaced road onto the coast path (dogs on lead here). The path soon goes close to the cliff edge. Go over a stile and through a gate and then keep to a well-defined path along the seaward edge of a steep field. The path becomes a grassy track leading towards houses on Chapel Point.

❸ Cross a surfaced drive and follow the coast path above Colona Beach. Go over a stile behind a boathouse and into a field. Turn right, immediately, alongside a stream.

🐾 ON THE WALK
The low coastline and rocky foreshore round Chapel Point and Colona Beach are ideal habitats for birds such as the turnstone. The turnstone is a smallish bird slightly bigger than a thrush. It has mottled brown feathers, a white front and orange legs and can be seen working very quickly along the shoreline and among seaweedy rocks looking for food with its very strong, pointed beak.

❹ Go through a gap in a hedge, then walk along the bottom of a second field and go through a gate into a field. Keep to the stream edge of the field.

❺ Go through a gate in front of a house and climb up some steps. Join a stony track and keep walking straight ahead through a gate and join a surfaced drive at Bodrugan Barton farm.

❻ Follow the drive through an entranceway to reach the public road. Turn right and descend steeply to reach Portmellon.

🍴 EATING AND DRINKING
The Rising Sun Inn at Portmellon is a classic Cornish hostelry where you can choose from a fine array of real ales and enjoy a pub lunch or a more substantial meal. Fish dishes are a specialty.

🌐 IN THE AREA
Nearby Mevagissey should not be missed, of course. A stroll around the harbour area and the older parts of the village is a pleasure in itself, but you should fit in visits to the Mevagissey Aquarium, housed in the old lifeboat house at the harbour, and to Mevagissey Museum, housed in an 18th-century building and full of splendid exhibits.

A WALK FROM REMOTE PORTLOE

Through the twists and turns
of a lonely coastline.

The tiny coastal village of Portloe is where you really step back in Cornish time. This is a part of Cornwall into which the modern world has not managed to bulldoze its way. The narrow lanes that eventually make their way to Portloe have little sympathy for large vehicles, so that Portloe has been spared too much focus as a tourist destination. The coast to either side of the village continues the remote theme. You move through a delightfully detached world where nothing matters so much as the wild beauty of the landscape

Unspoiled Village

The poet John Betjeman thought Portloe was one of the most unspoiled villages in Cornwall and would be delighted to see that it remains so to this day. A century ago over 50 fishing boats worked from this sheltered cove. Today there is only a handful but they keep a powerful tradition of great seamanship and local knowledge alive. Portloe does not go unnoticed however. With its lovely traditional houses and compelling location within a niche in the cliffs, the village is also a favourite with filmmakers. Walt Disney shot scenes for the 1949 version of *Treasure Island* here while the television dramatisation of the novel *The Camomile Lawn* was shot at a nearby house. Portloe has even doubled for Ireland in a feature film and appeared in several other productions.

Cheerful Meander

The first section of the coast path that you follow out of Portloe is a cheerful meander up and down steps and around quaint cottages and even across the slipway of the old Portloe lifeboathouse. The path climbs to what must be one of the National Trust's tiniest properties, The Flagstaff, a small walled-in patch of land where a revenue lookout was established during the heyday of Cornish smuggling, for which Portloe had a certain reputation. Beyond here is a later coastguard building now disused. The return route through quiet inland fields back to Portloe underpins this charming sense of remoteness.

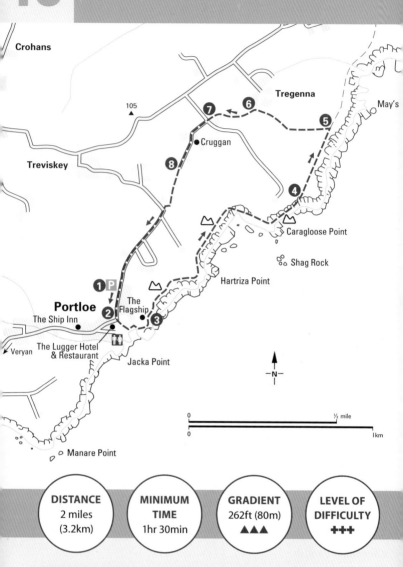

Crohans

105 ▲

Treviskey

Tregenna

May's

7

6

5

● Cruggan

8

4

Caragloose Point

⌂

⌂

Shag Rock ஃ

⌂

Hartriza Point

1 P

Portloe

2 The Flagship

The Ship Inn ●

3

The Lugger Hotel & Restaurant

↙ Veryan

Jacka Point

→N←

Manare Point ◌

| 0 | ½ mile |
| 0 | 1 km |

DISTANCE	MINIMUM TIME	GRADIENT	LEVEL OF DIFFICULTY
2 miles (3.2km)	1hr 30min	262ft (80m) ▲▲▲	+++

PATHS Well defined on coastal section but are steep and rocky in places and can be muddy and quite slippery during very wet weather. Paths through fields are not always well defined; 4 stiles, 2 of which are very high **LANDSCAPE** Low but rugged and undulating coastline with flat fields inland on higher ground **SUGGESTED MAP** OS Explorer 105 Falmouth & Mevagissey **START/FINISH** Grid reference: SW 938396 **DOG FRIENDLINESS** Dogs on lead through fields and by houses **PARKING** Portloe **PUBLIC TOILETS** Above south side of Portloe Harbour

WALK 16 DIRECTIONS

❶ Leave the car park and turn right and downhill towards Portloe. Go left through a gapway just round a bend in the road and descend some rock steps and then steeper concrete steps.

❷ Turn left at a junction with the coast path. Descend steps and step awkwardly across a little stream. Bear left across the slipway of the one-time lifeboat station, and then go up very steep steps. Turn left up more steps and then turn right up a railed walkway. Bear round right in front of a row of cottages and then up steep steps.

❸ Pass The Flagstaff and then pass a disused Coastguard lookout and continue along the coast path through a number of steep sections to reach Caragloose Point. Continue to the National Trust property of Tregenna.

❹ Climb more steep steps and then a very steep and rocky section. Go through a wooden kissing gate (dogs on lead here) and then through another kissing gate. Continue along a level path high above the sea with an open field inland. Pass a section of windswept blackthorns and sycamores.

❺ A few paces before a wooden kissing gate go sharply left up an earthy path into the open field above. Follow a faint, grassy path slightly leftwards across the field. This is a National Trust permissive path. Go through a wooden kissing gate and along the left edge of a field to another kissing gate and then follow a muddy track towards houses at Tregenna.

❻ Just before a gate and stile at Tregenna, turn sharply left along the field-edge to reach a stile. Go over the stile and head for the far right-hand corner of the next field. Go over a wooden barrier with a V-shaped slot, climb over a high slate stile and turn left along a field-edge to a metal gate.

🍴 EATING AND DRINKING

The Lugger Hotel, once owned by a 19th-century smuggler, has a formidable culinary reputation, especially for its seafood. The Ship Inn is located above the harbour and lives up to its name with its nautical décor. Snacks, lunches and evening meals are available.

---

❼ There is a very steep stile on the left, but it is difficult to negotiate. It is better to go through the gate. Go down the concrete farm track and follow it as it bears left through Cruggan farm and then bends to the right down a hedged-in lane.

❽ Go through a gateway, or over a stile to its right, and bear slightly right across the middle of a field towards a bungalow. Go through a metal kissing gate onto a public road and turn left to return to the car park at Portloe.

ABOVE THE SEA AT PARK HEAD

Exploring the spectacular coastal landscape
at Park Head and Bedruthan Steps.

The flat, unremarkable countryside that lies inland from Bedruthan Steps belies the stupendous nature of the area's coastline geology. Green fields run almost to the sliced-off edges of 300ft (91m) cliffs. At the foot of the cliffs lie dramatic rock islands which at high tide are battered by crashing waves and at low tide, stand in dramatic isolation, rooted in an expanse of sea-stained sand. The islands, or stacks, are portrayed as being the stepping stones of a legendary giant called Bedruthan, but this conceit only blew in with Victorian tourists.

Less Crowded

This walk takes you to the quieter northern end of the Bedruthan area, at Park Head, an area less crowded than that around Carnewas to the south. The walk is on National Trust property and first takes you easily along the southern rim of the Porth Mear valley to the start of Park Head's corrugated coastline. At the coast you can divert from the main route down to the peaceful Porth Mear Cove where there are rock pools enough to keep a whole family entertained for half the morning. The cliffs at Park Head have the same dramatic convolutions as those at Bedruthan. There are no offshore pinnacles here, but landslips, rock arches and twisted bands of rock make these cliffs just as fantastic. As always you must be very careful if peering over cliff edges.

Inland from the cliffs are fields enclosed by handsome slate 'hedges' furred with lichen and dotted with cushions of pink thrift. The distinctive herringbone pattern of these hedges seems to replicate the geology and texture of the cliffs themselves, a reflection of how much traditional human skills and natural materials can harmonise with landscape. You are walking always in the footsteps of ancient peoples here. Read the landscape around you as you head south towards Park Head itself and you'll spot several grassy mounds. These are Bronze Age burial sites or barrows and they suggest that the Park Head area was an important landscape, even in prehistoric times. At Park Head itself, you pass through the protective embankments of an Iron Age settlement that once occupied the crown of the headland.

Opposite: Golden sand at Bedruthan Steps, near Newquay

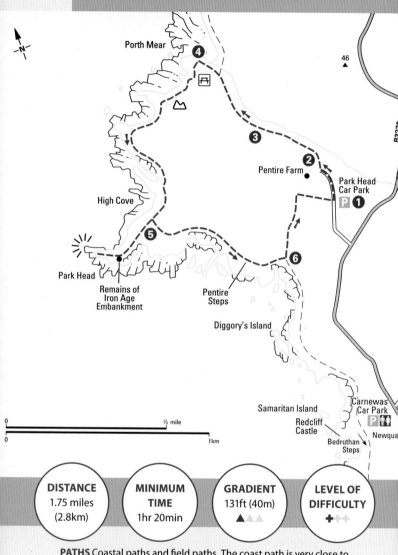

| | DISTANCE
1.75 miles
(2.8km) | MINIMUM
TIME
1hr 20min | GRADIENT
131ft (40m)
▲▲▲ | LEVEL OF
DIFFICULTY
+++ |

PATHS Coastal paths and field paths. The coast path is very close to unguarded cliff edges in some places; take care in windy weather; watch children and dogs if near cliff edges; 1 stile **LANDSCAPE** Spectacular cliffs and dramatic sea stacks **SUGGESTED MAP** OS Explorer 106 Newquay and Padstow
START/FINISH Grid reference: SW 852707
DOG FRIENDLINESS Dogs on lead through grazed areas
PARKING National Trust Parkhead car park
PUBLIC TOILETS Carnewas car park SW 850691

WALK 17 DIRECTIONS

❶ Leave the car park at its seaward end and follow a lane towards Pentire Farm. Just before a house go through a gate on the right, signposted 'Porthmear Beach and Park Head'.

❷ Keep to the left-hand edge of a field and then go over a wooden stile by a gateway. Bear diagonally right down the next field and go through a gate in its bottom corner.

❸ Keep left where the path forks and cross a wooden boardwalk.

🐦 ON THE WALK

Along the tops of the cliffs watch for the silent, unflappable flight of the stubby-winged fulmar as it glides on thermals just off the edges of the cliffs. The fulmar has two small holes on its upper beak through which it ejects a foul-smelling green liquid at predators. Don't get too close.

🍴 EATING AND DRINKING

There are no refreshment opportunities on the route, but the National Trust Tea Room at Carnewas car park offers cream teas, light snacks and drinks. It is open for most of the year, except from about mid-December to mid-February.

❹ Join the coast path above the attractive Porth Mear cove. Descend to the cove if you wish. On the main route, go through a kissing gate and continue steadily uphill along the coast path and continue to the promontory of Park Head. (Take great care near the cliff edges.)

❺ At Park Head, you can walk out to the top of the promontory. On the main route follow the grassy coast path south passing through a wide gap in a herringbone pattern 'slate wall. Follow the path close to the cliff edge. Reach the corner of a field wall and keep parallel to the wall to a kissing gate.

❻ Go through the kissing gate and follow a permissive footpath along field-edges. Just before the farm turn right and go through two fields to reach the car park.

🏞 IN THE AREA

A descent of the cliff staircase to Bedruthan Beach should not be missed. The entrance to the staircase is at Carnewas, a mile (1.6km) south from the Pentire car park. The staircase has been well secured by the National Trust. The steps are steep enough, however and there are 139 of them – or thereabouts. The staircase is closed to the public from November to the end of February. Be careful on the rocky sections of Bedruthan Beach where it can be very slippery. At low tide you can explore the beach, but be very aware of tide times; the flooding tide can cut you off very quickly. The day's tide times are usually displayed at the top of the staircase. Swimming from Bedruthan Beach is not advised.

PENTIRE POINT WEST

A short walk round the 'Sand Country'
of Crantock and Pentire Point West.

South of Newquay is genuine 'Sand Country' where vast swathes of sand
sprawl across the beaches at Crantock, Holywell Beach and especially
at Penhale and Perran Beach, making this part of North Cornwall a
holidaymaker's heaven and a surfer's paradise.

Legends

These vast acres of sand have brought their own legends and none so
enduring than the story of Langarrow, a fantastical city of great wealth and
loose living that once occupied the coast. There is a flavour of biblical wrath
here as Langarrow is said to have been so decadent that the hand of God
raised huge wind storms that buried the city and its inhabitants under tons
of sand. On Perranporth beach and the dunes to the south there is certainly
historical evidence of a dramatic shifting of sand. It was here that Cornwall's
patron saint, Piran, is said to have drifted ashore on a millstone that carried
him across the sea from Ireland, sometime in the 5th or 6th century AD.

Historic Area

This walk takes you round the isolated headland of Pentire Point West
overlooking Crantock Beach to the east. Midway on the walk is the charming
bonus of Porth Joke, or Polly Joke, a deep inlet that culminates at a lovely
beach; so take your swimming kit but be aware that the tide advances quickly
here. The name 'Joke' is said to be a corruption of the Cornish word *gwic*
which means a creek or inlet. Some claim it derives from the term 'chough'
although the Cornish name for jackdaw has a stronger claim. The slopes
to either side of Porth Joke are a mass of colourful wild flowers in spring
and summer. The last section of the walk leads past an area of sand-dusted
grasslands and fields known as The Kelseys, a historic area of land enclosures
that date from medieval times and which have fascinating names, such as
Beef Park and Jawbone Pitt Park. These grasslands are naturally fertilised by
the windblown sand and are noted for their good grazing. Today, the Kelseys
are in the care of the National Trust and are still grazed at times.

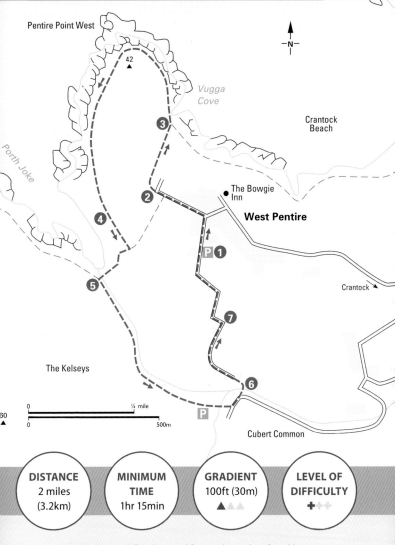

Pentire Point West

42 ▲

Vugga Cove

3

Crantock Beach

2

● The Bowgie Inn

West Pentire

4

Porth Joke

P 1

Crantock ►

5

7

Crantock ►

The Kelseys

6

0 ¼ mile
0 500m

60 ▲

P

Cubert Common

DISTANCE	MINIMUM TIME	GRADIENT	LEVEL OF DIFFICULTY
2 miles (3.2km)	1hr 15min	100ft (30m) ▲▲▲	✚✚✚

PATHS Clearly defined coastal footpaths and surfaced lanes
LANDSCAPE Green and grassy clifftops above sandy beaches
SUGGESTED MAP OS Explorer 104 Redruth & St Agnes
START/FINISH Grid reference: SW 777604
DOG FRIENDLINESS On lead through areas of potential grazing
PARKING West Pentire
PUBLIC TOILETS Crantock village

WALK 18 DIRECTIONS

❶ Leave the car park by its entrance and walk directly down the approach road. In 20yds (18m) turn left, signposted 'To Polly Joke', go through a kissing gate and continue along the track ahead.

❷ Keep straight ahead at a fork and, in 20yds (18m), take the narrow path to the right just before a wooden gate and soon join the coast path.

❸ Turn left and immediately go through a kissing gate. Follow a grassy track round the headland of Pentire Point West, keeping left at a crossing of paths. Follow the cliff edge along the side of Porth Joke.

🌿 ON THE WALK
Typical plants that flourish on sandy soil include the deep-rooting sea rocket, a straggling ground plant with green fleshy leaves and pale lilac flowers. Look for the distinctive sea holly with its spiky blue-green leaves and sky-blue flowers, and sea bindweed, which has fleshy kidney-shaped leaves, and pink and white trumpet-shaped flowers.

🍽 EATING AND DRINKING
The Bowgie Inn is just down from the car park and has a grand position overlooking Crantock Bay. There's a wide-ranging menu, including pub lunches and sandwiches as well as full main meals.

❹ Go through a kissing gate and soon join another path. Keep right and go through a kissing gate and cross a plank bridge at the head of the beach.

❺ Turn left off the coast path, signposted 'Cubert Common', and follow a sandy path and go through a gate. Continue to another gate into a car park. Keep straight ahead and leave the car park via a wooden stile next to the car park entrance.

❻ Keep left on a stony track and in about 25yds (23m) go through a wooden kissing gate on the left and onto a fenced path alongside a field.

❼ Cross a wooden bridge and soon meet a surfaced road. Turn left and follow the road back to the start point car park.

🌍 IN THE AREA
Nearby Crantock is a charming village and the partly 14th-century Church of St Carantock is worth a visit. At the very heart of the village is the serene little Round Garden, now in the care of the National Trust and once thought to be the site of a Celtic Christian chapel although a one-time use as a traditional livestock pound is also likely.

A WALK THROUGH THE BISHOP'S WOOD

A short and gentle stroll through the richly diverse
woodlands of a forestry estate near Truro.

Going down to the woods in Cornwall is always a delightful antidote to the
county's surfeit of sea. Coastal woodlands do not always offer such an escape;
views of the sea, the sound of the sea, and even the smell of the sea keep
intruding. At leafy enclaves such as Bishop's Wood near Truro, however, you
can safely bury the anchor deep inland.

The walk starts from the forestry car park at the south end of the woods
and leads along its eastern edge through Lady's Wood, on a track that is
wonderfully eerie and enclosed. A robust little stream runs below the track.
Beech trees dominate here and further into the wood, oak, hazel, birch,
Japanese larch and holly lie to either side of the track.

The track leads on to the top end of the wood just before Lanner Mill. Here
you turn uphill and on to a broad forestry ride that leads back south along
the higher ridge of the woods. Half-way along you can divert left from the
track to visit the site of the Iron Age settlement. The large bank and ditch
that encircled the site is still visible. This is a well-preserved site, although the
trees and scrub blur the impact of the large bank and ditch construction.
Such hilltop sites date from between the Bronze and Iron Ages and reflect
a growing territorialism.

Commercial Centres

These were not forts in the narrow sense of being built purely for defence.
They were defensible sites, certainly, but they were commercial and cultural
centres as much as anything else, being the focus of a large territory of
scattered farmsteads and settlements from which the unforested hilltop site
would be easily seen. The hilltop 'fort' or 'castle' represented a central refuge
in times of trouble, but served also as a place to bring livestock to market and
to exchange household goods and to socialise and celebrate.

From the Iron Age site, the last part of the walk takes you on to even higher
ground and through newly planted conifers; the young trees are still low
enough to afford a distant glimpse of the elegant spires of Truro's cathedral,
a fitting view from a Bishop's Wood.

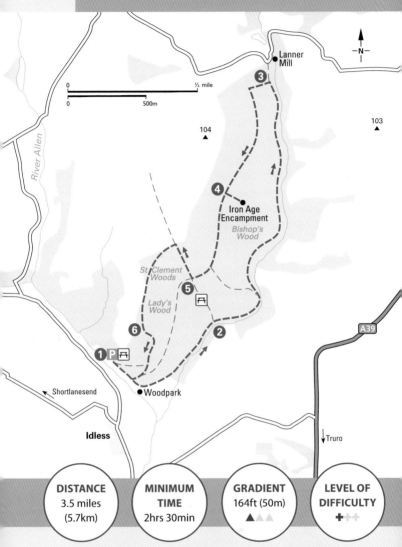

DISTANCE	MINIMUM TIME	GRADIENT	LEVEL OF DIFFICULTY
3.5 miles (5.7km)	2hrs 30min	164ft (50m) ▲▲▲	✚✚✚

PATHS Forest tracks and paths. Can be very muddy after rain
LANDSCAPE Mixed woodland **SUGGESTED MAP** OS Explorer 105 Falmouth
& Mevagissey **START/FINISH** Grid reference: SW 821478
DOG FRIENDLINESS Dogs are welcomed throughout the woods. The authorities
ask that owners clear up their dog's mess in the car park and first sections of forest
tracks **PARKING** Forestry car park, north of Idless, near Truro
PUBLIC TOILETS None on route **NOTE** Car park gates are closed at sunset.
Working woodland, please take note of notices advising work in progress

WALK 19 DIRECTIONS

❶ Leave the top end of the car park via the wooden barrier and go along a broad track. In a few paces at a fork, keep to the right fork and follow the track above Woodpark and along the inside edge of the wood. This track can be very muddy after rain.

❷ Keep ahead on the main track, walking parallel to the river, ignoring branch tracks leading off to the left.

❸ Just before the northern end of the wood you reach a fork. Keep to the main track as it bends left and uphill. The track levels off and at an open area merges with a broad forestry ride. Keep ahead along this ride.

❹ At a notice indiating the site of the remains of an Iron Age encampment, go left along a path beneath conifer trees to reach the bank and ditch of the encampment. Return to the main track and turn left.

❺ At a bend beside a wooden bench, where tracks lead off to left and right, go right and follow a public footpath uphill. At a path crossing turn left and follow the path through scrubland and young pine trees.

❻ Re-enter mature woodland and follow a track downhill. Keep right at a junction, then go left at the next junction. Reach a T-junction with a broad track. Turn right and follow the track back to the car park.

🐾 ON THE WALK

Old woods are often rich in fungi. Look for the trunks of dead trees and you may find the great plate-like layers of various bracket fungi. Other fungi to look for among the rich humus of the woodland underlayer are stinkhorn fungus, the rudely unmistakable *Phallus impudicus*. On oak trees you may find little round wood-like growths known popularly as 'oak apples'. These are produced by gall wasps laying their eggs on oak leaves. The oak apple grows round the egg to protect it during incubation. Look closely and you may see a tiny hole where the adult insect has emerged.

EXPLORING TRURO'S HERITAGE

A pleasant walk between the old
and new in Cornwall's capital city.

This easygoing route takes you past some of Truro's finest buildings and is a
pleasant contrast to Cornwall's coastline. Truro is an easy place to get around.
Its central area is generally flat and the city as a whole has the character of a
large market town rather than a city. Relax and stroll at your leisure…

Georgian Buildings

For a time during the late 18th century Truro's Georgian buildings were a fair
match for some of the lesser buildings of Bath and were indeed built using
honey-coloured Bath stone. Today Truro's landmark building is its cathedral,
whose soaring central spire can be seen from all round the city. The cathedral
is relatively modern, relative that is to most British cathedrals, and was built
between 1880 and 1910. Its style is Early English Gothic, although the design
of its three great spires reflects a French influence.

Museum

Truro's splendid cathedral apart, the walk takes you to the Royal Cornwall
Museum and on to the endearing early 19th-century Walsingham Place
whose left-hand terrace sports cheerful lion's head corbels on the doorcases.
Lemon Street is next, a wide avenue of Georgian houses that were built
during the late 18th century when Truro was the commercial, political
and cultural centre of Cornwall. The walk then takes you to the semi-
pedestrianised Lemon Quay and Back Quay where the Hall for Cornwall is
the cultural focus of the city. Truro's central street is the very wide Boscawen
Street. In 1797 the medieval chaos of the Boscawen Street area was swept
away and today's broad, cobbled space was created. If traffic were banished
from Boscawen Street it would take on the character of a truly European
market square. The walk leads past the Gothic Coinage Hall at the head of
Boscawen Street and meanders alongside the tiny River Allen back towards
the cathedral and past some iconic buildings, not least the Public Library in
Union Place. In the spaces between all of these fine buildings modern Truro
bustles along as Cornwall's major shopping and administrative centre.

Opposite: Quaint streets overlooked by Truro Cathedral   Truro   75

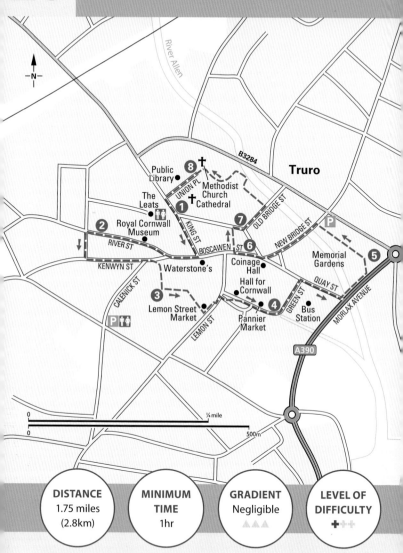

DISTANCE	MINIMUM TIME	GRADIENT	LEVEL OF DIFFICULTY
1.75 miles (2.8km)	1hr	Negligible ▲▲▲	✚✚✚

PATHS Surfaced pavements and walkways throughout **LANDSCAPE** Cityscape **SUGGESTED MAP** City of Truro official map available from Tourist Information Centre, Municipal Buildings, Boscawen Street **START/FINISH** Grid reference: SW 826448 **DOG FRIENDLINESS** Dogs should be kept under control. Dog fouling regulations are strictly enforced **PARKING** There are public car parks in Old Bridge Street and on Calenick Street. A park-and-ride service to the city centre operates from a car park on the A390 just outside the city to the west **PUBLIC TOILETS** At the Calenick multi-storey car park and in The Leats, opposite High Cross

WALK 20 DIRECTIONS

1 Start beside High Cross, the tall Celtic stone cross in front of Truro Cathedral. Turn left down King Street and at a junction with Boscawen Street, turn right. Keep right at the next junction and go along River Street to the Royal Cornwall Museum.

2 Keep along River Street to a cross-roads. Cross left, with care and go down Little Castle Street. Turn left at a T-junction and go along Kenwyn Street. Keep to the right, past a junction with Calenick Street, and then turn right at the next junction, keeping left where it forks. Go down Walsingham Place.

3 Turn left at a junction and in a few paces go through the Lemon Street Market. Walk beneath a granite archway into Lemon Street. Cross the road, turn left and then turn right into Lemon Quay. Cross the pedestrianised area and turn right past the Hall for Cornwall and the Pannier Market.

4 Turn left into Green Street, opposite the bus station. Turn right at a junction and go down Quay Street. Turn left at the next junction with the busy Morlaix Avenue and cross a bridge over the narrow River Allen. Turn left just before a big roundabout and go down a railed walkway by a 'Subway' sign.

5 Bear right and then left and walk through the Memorial Gardens alongside the River Allen. keep going

> **🍴 EATING AND DRINKING**
>
> Truro is well served by cafés, restaurants and pubs. The Gallery Café in the Lemon Street Market (see Point **3**) offers excellent lunches and meals, with exhibitions of paintings adding to the experience.

past houses and emerge on New Bridge Street with a fine view of the cathedral ahead. Turn left over a bridge and keep left, where the road forks, to go along Duke Street and into the wide Boscawen Street by the Coinage Hall.

6 Keep along the right-hand side of Boscawen Street then turn right down Cathedral Lane. Cross at a junction and turn right alongside the old walls of the 16th-century Church of St Mary, now part of the cathedral.

7 Turn left down Old Bridge Street and left again along the narrow Wilkes Way alongside the River Allen. Bear round left at a junction and continue with the cathedral on your left. Note the great rose window. Pass the old Truro Cathedral School, keep right at a fork and then go left at a junction.

8 Cross a small cobbled area in front of the handsome building of the Methodist Church and continue along the cobbled Union Place alongside the city library. Reach a junction with Pydar Street and turn left to reach High Cross and the cathedral.

THE WATER WORLD OF ROSELAND

A delightful walk on one of
Cornwall's loveliest peninsulas.

You never feel crowded on the Roseland Peninsula, a long narrow promontory of land that seems to replicate a larger Cornwall, where the influence of the sea dominates but never overwhelms. It enjoys a wonderful sense of detachment from the outside world and its villages and hamlets are not swamped by too much traffic or by too many visitors.

Deep Woods and Wooded Banks

The peninsula is a graceful mix of green fields and deep woods, dotted with small farms and villages, seawashed on its eastern shore and lapped by the waters of the estuary of the River Fal and its tidal creeks on its western side. This walk takes you deep into the tree-shrouded world of the Percuil River, which divides the southern end of Roseland into two, one arm terminating at St Anthony Head on the east and St Mawes on the west. The Percuil curls lazily between lush green banks its final muddy fingers probing deep inland at Polingey Creek and Trethem Creek while random inlets create even smaller peninsulas. The walk leads you down from the high ground of the Roseland, at the village of Gerrans, to the Pelyn Creek and to the riverside hamlet of Percuil, a yachting and boating centre.

From Percuil, the walk skirts the edges of the Percuil River where, at low water, great swathes of mud are exposed between the wooded banks only to disappear beneath shining water at high tide. Yachts and motor boats swing gently on their moorings or sit like stranded birds on the mudbanks. The path makes a final turn alongside Polingey Creek where you can see the remains of a stone causeway that crossed the head of the creek. This was part of a once busy world of tidal milling whereby sea water would be impounded at high tide and then used to power mill machinery. There was a mill building here, probably from the medieval period and milling was reported as being carried out until well into the 19th century. Seagoing-vessels once berthed at a small quay at Pelingey and at Percuil, carrying goods and materials. From the head of Pelingey Creek your route takes you back to Gerrans along a typical sunken lane that would have been a major thoroughfare in the old days.

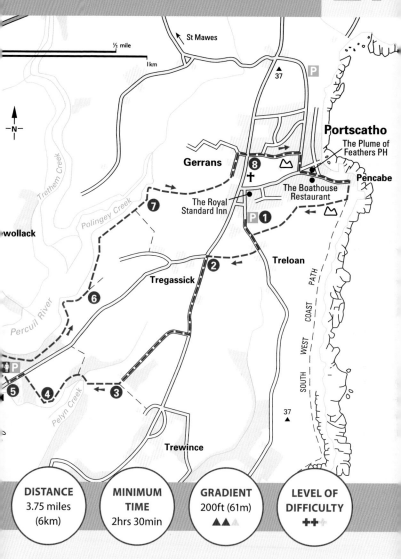

½ mile
1 km

St Mawes

—N—

▲ 37

Portscatho
The Plume of
Feathers PH

Gerrans

Trethem Creek

Polingey Creek

⑧ ⛪

⌂

The Boathouse
Restaurant

Pencabe

wollack

⑦

The Royal
Standard Inn

Ⓟ ❶

⌂

Treloan

②

Tregassick

Percuil River

⑥

SOUTH WEST COAST PATH

Ⓟ

⑤ ④ ③

Pelyn Creek

▲ 37

Trewince

DISTANCE	MINIMUM TIME	GRADIENT	LEVEL OF DIFFICULTY
3.75 miles (6km)	2hrs 30min	200ft (61m) ▲▲△	++✛

PATHS Excellent throughout, but can be very muddy in wet conditions
and during winter; 8 stiles **LANDSCAPE** A coastal peninsula with open sea on
one side and tree-lined tidal creeks on the other **SUGGESTED MAP** OS Explorer
105 Falmouth & Mevagissey **START/FINISH** Grid reference: SW 873350
DOG FRIENDLINESS Dogs on lead through fields and by houses
PARKING Gerrans free car park
PUBLIC TOILETS Percuil and Portscatho

WALK 21 DIRECTIONS

❶ Leave the car park and turn left down a narrow lane. Just past the entrance to Treloan Caravan Park turn off right, signposted to Percuil. Go over a steep stile and, in a few paces, go through a kissing gate and follow the path across two fields and two stiles to reach a public road.

❷ Turn left and after a 0.25 miles (400m), turn off right along a wide track, signposted 'Pelyn Creek'. Cross a cattle grid and go through a gate and follow a partly concreted drive (dogs on lead here). Cross another cattle grid and keep straight ahead past a house and along a muddy track.

❸ Go over a high slate stile by a gate and follow a path round the edge of a field. Cross a stile and reach the head of Pelyn Creek. Turn right across the head of the creek and go through a wooden gate onto the National Trust property of Percuil. Turn left at a junction and follow a wide grassy track.

❹ Go through a gate by a bench and follow a field-edge. Go through another gate and follow a woodland track to reach a narrow public lane. Turn left and downhill to Percuil.

❺ Turn right into the lower entrance of the Percuil car park. Go past the toilets and through a gap in the car park's top left-hand corner. Keep alongside a fence, go through a gate and follow a tree-shaded track. At a fork keep left, through a kissing gate and follow the path through fields and hedged areas.

❻ Keep ahead at a not too obvious fork in the path beside some trees. Ignore the path leading uphill to the right. Cross a ramp and stile and follow the left edge of a field. Go through a gate into woods. Keep on at a junction, signed 'Gerrans', and follow a path alongside Polingey Creek.

> ⓧ **EATING AND DRINKING**
> The Royal Standard Inn at Gerrans has a good varied menu. At Portscatho there's tasty pub food at The Plume of Feathers in the square while The Boathouse restaurant opposite has a charming garden area, is licensed and has excellent food.

❼ Beyond the head of the creek, go over a stone stile and a wooden bridge. Go over a stile and down steps to bear right along a sunken lane. Join a driveway by a house, turn right at a junction and reach the public road at Gerrans. (A right turn towards Gerrans church leads back to the car park.)

❽ Cross the road diagonally right and go left on a walkway to a main road. Turn right into Portscatho. Follow the road to the end of the village and join the coast path. Turn right at the first junction and follow field paths uphill. Reach a gate into a tree-shaded lane. At a road turn right to the car park.

A WATERSIDE WALK BY THE FAL ESTUARY

From Mylor Churchtown to Flushing in a quiet peninsular world still dominated by ships and sails.

The inner estuary of the River Fal, the Carrick Roads, is reputedly the third largest natural harbour in the world. It has welcomed all manner of vessels, from Tudor warships to fishing fleets, to modern cargo vessels and oil rigs and a growing number of yachts. Part of the long maritime heritage of the Fal belongs to the Post Office Packet Service that was responsible for communications throughout the British Empire. The Packet Service was based in the Fal from 1689 to 1850. It was a glorious and freebooting period of British seafaring. Fast Packet vessels ran south to Spain and Portugal and then on to the Americas. The Packet sailors were notorious for their opportunism and many a Packet ship returned from a trip with more than half its cargo as contraband goods. The main Packet base was at Falmouth, but Mylor was a servicing and victualling yard for the Packet boats and many of the Packet captains lived at Flushing in what was effectively maritime suburbia.

At Mylor today, maritime traditions are as strong as ever, as far as leisure sailing goes. Boatyards still bustle with work and local sailing clubs thrive. A gold medal winner in sailing at the 2000 Olympics in Australia, Ben Ainslie learned many of his skills as a Laser dinghy sailor in these waters and today every creek and inlet of the Fal is dense with sailing and leisure craft.

Wooded Valley

The walk takes you from Mylor along the shores of the blunt headland between Mylor Creek and the Penryn River and on to Flushing, in full view of Falmouth docks and waterfront. Flushing is an enclave of handsome houses, many with distinctly Dutch features. At Point ❹ on the walk, note the plaque opposite, commemorating the Post Office Packet Service. From Flushing you turn inland and on to a delightful old track that runs down a wooded valley to the tree-shrouded waters of Mylor Creek from where quiet lanes lead back to St Mylor Church. Here in a churchyard that resonates with maritime history, stands the Ganges Memorial erected in 1872, a commemoration of 53 youngsters who died, mainly of disease, on the famous Royal Naval training ship HMS *Ganges* that was based at Mylor from 1866 to 1899.

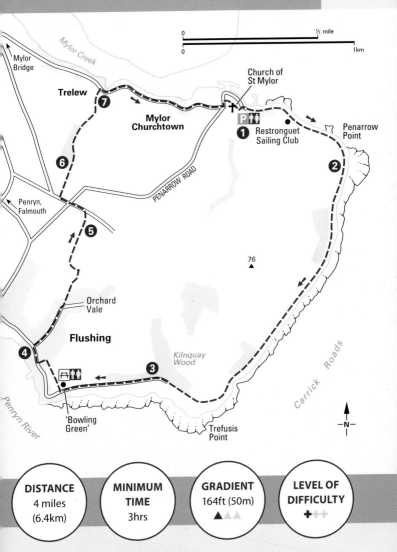

DISTANCE
4 miles
(6.4km)

MINIMUM TIME
3hrs

GRADIENT
164ft (50m)
▲ ▲ ▲

LEVEL OF DIFFICULTY
✚ ✚ ✚

PATHS Good paths throughout. Wooded section to Trelew Farm is often very wet, 7 stiles **LANDSCAPE** Wooded peninsula flanked by river estuaries and creeks **SUGGESTED MAP** OS Explorer 105 Falmouth & Mevagissey
START/FINISH Grid reference: SW 821352
DOG FRIENDLINESS Dogs on lead through grazed areas
PARKING Mylor Churchtown car park
PUBLIC TOILETS Mylor Churchtown and Flushing

Opposite: Stile on the coastal route from Trefusis Point   Mylor   **83**

WALK 22 DIRECTIONS

❶ From the car park entrance, turn right to reach the start of a surfaced lane, signposted to Flushing. Follow the lane, then, by the gateway of a house, bear left along a path. Pass in front of Restronguet Sailing Club and keep to the right of a detached building.

❷ Follow the path round Penarrow Point and continue round Trefusis Point. Reach a gate and granite grid stile by a wooden shack at Kilnquay Wood. Continue until your reach a lane.

❸ Follow the surfaced lane round left, then go right through a gap beside a gate and continue along a public road. Where the road drops down towards the water's edge, bear right up a surfaced slope to the grassy area of the 'Bowling Green'. (Strictly no dog fouling, please.) Continue past a little pavilion and toilets and go down a surfaced path, then turn left at a junction just after passing two seats.

❹ Turn right at a street junction and go past the Seven Stars Inn. At a junction by the Royal Standard Inn, keep right and go up Kersey Road. At the top of the road, by Orchard Vale, go left up steps, signposted 'Mylor Church'. Cross a stile and keep to the field-edge to reach an isolated house and to a stile made of granite bollards.

❺ In 25yds (23m) go right, through a gate then turn left over a cattle grid and follow the drive to a public road, Penarrow Road. Cross with care and go down the road opposite for 30yds (27m), then go right down steps and on down the field-edge.

❻ Enter woodland and keep right at a junction to follow a rocky path that is often a mini stream after heavy rainfall. Go through a gate, keep ahead at a junction then cross a small stream. Go through a tiny gate and then turn right down a farm track to reach a surfaced lane at Trelew.

> **🍴 EATING AND DRINKING**
> Half-way through the route, at Flushing, there are two good pubs, the Seven Stars Inn and the Royal Standard Inn. At Mylor Bridge, you'll find the Castaways restaurant and also Café Mylor.

❼ Turn right along the lane, passing an old water pump. When you get to a slipway, keep ahead along the unsurfaced track. Continue along between granite posts and on to join the public road into Mylor Churchtown. Cross the road with care (this is a blind corner) and go through the churchyard of St Mylor Church (please note, the path through the churchyard is not a public right of way). Turn right when you reach the waterfront to find the car park in Mylor Churchtown.

CHAPEL PORTH'S WILD FLOWER HABITATS

A walk through the wildlife habitats of clifftop mine workings, maritime heathland and wooded valley.

The area surrounding the seaside village of St Agnes and its neighbouring cove of Chapel Porth has a dramatic history of tin and copper mining. Even the car park at Chapel Porth, from where this walk begins, was once crammed full of mine buildings and industrial activity during the 19th century. Chapel Coombe, the tranquil and deeply vegetated stream valley behind the cove was once wreathed in smoke and rang with the sounds of mine processing.

Scarred Ground

In spite of all this industrial activity it is only on the cliff top, through which the first section of the walk passes, that you see the scarred ground, the spoil heaps and ruined walls of Victorian mining. Much of the area is now in the care of the National Trust and perhaps the most surprising aspect of this landscape is that it is of national importance for its wild flowers and plants because of its designation as a classic coastal heath and maritime habitat. Windblown sand carried up from the long swathes of beach below the cliffs enriches the soil with natural lime, the perfect environment for a myriad of plants such as low-lying heath bedstraw and thyme. Heath bedstraw is identified by its small spear-shaped leaves and tiny white flowers. Thyme has small dark green leaves and tight clusters of purple-pink flowers.

Beautiful Mosaic

On the heathland behind the cliffs, bell heather, cross-leafed heath and western gorse hold sway; their mix of purple and yellow flowers makes a beautiful mosaic of colour, especially during autumn. In this kind of habitat you should also spot the tiny yellow-headed tormentil and the blue-flowered milkwort. The lovely heath spotted orchid also grows amid the heather and gorse as does eyebright with its small but distinctive purple-veined white flowers. The moods of the weather play their part in the atmosphere of these wide open cliff tops. It is an exhilarating experience to walk along these cliffs and then to enjoy the contrast of the peace and quiet amid the sheltering trees of the Chapel Coombe valley.

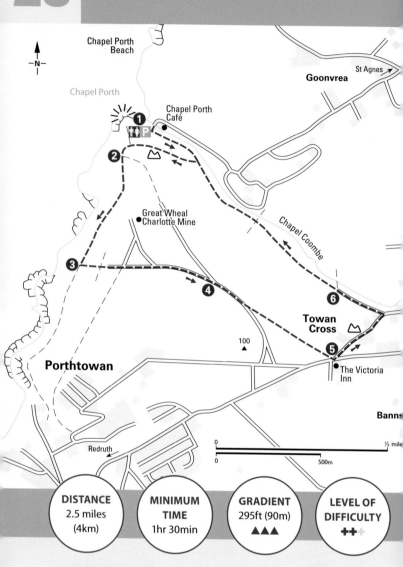

DISTANCE
2.5 miles
(4km)

MINIMUM
TIME
1hr 30min

GRADIENT
295ft (90m)
▲▲▲

LEVEL OF
DIFFICULTY
++÷

PATHS Stony underfoot on cliff top, otherwise good. May be muddy
in valley bottom **LANDSCAPE** Dramatic, but desolate, mining landscape
and lush green valley **SUGGESTED MAP** OS Explorer 104 Redruth & St Agnes
START/FINISH Grid reference: SW 697495 **DOG FRIENDLINESS** Off lead but
under control **PARKING** National Trust car park Chapel Porth (free)
PUBLIC TOILETS Chapel Porth car park **NOTE** On one short coastal section, the
path is close to the edge of unfenced cliff. Take care of young children and dogs

WALK 23 DIRECTIONS

❶ From the back of the car park cross a wooden bridge over a stream and follow a path inland alongside the stream. At a junction, in about 0.25 miles (400m), turn sharply right and follow a stony track uphill. At a junction of tracks (acorn signpost), on the cliff top, keep ahead through waste heaps.

❷ Follow the track down left and then right, below the ruins of Great Wheal Charlotte mine stack. Keep ahead along the coast path. Take care of young children and dogs at a short section near the unfenced cliff edge.

❸ The coast path reaches a junction with a path coming in at an angle from the left. Turn sharply left here and follow a narrow path that runs directly inland. Reach a junction with a broad track. Keep across and along a wide track. Keep ahead at a cross-junction and bear right at the next junction.

❹ Turn right along a wide stony track at the next junction. Reach another junction and bear off left along a subsidiary track. Soon houses come into view and the public road is reached opposite The Victory Inn.

❺ Turn left across a la-yby and a grassy verge, opposite The Victory Inn and bear left down a surfaced lane. Descend quite steeply (watch for any traffic on narrow sections). Where the lane reaches the valley bottom, turn off left along a shaded, unsurfaced lane.

> ### ⌖ IN THE AREA
> Go for a stroll on the beach at Chapel Porth but, be warned, this is a tidal beach and the incoming tide can cover it very rapidly. Check for details on notices and with lifeguards. You should never enter any caves at the base of the cliffs. The village of St Agnes is near by and rewards a visit. Call in at the entertaining St Agnes Museum.

❻ At a junction with a path, bear off left and keep to the path along the tree filled valley to return to the car park at Chapel Porth.

> ### ♗ ON THE WALK
> During the summer months butterflies can be spotted along the sea cliffs and on the coastland heathland. You may spot the painted lady and the grayling, a brown butterfly, which has black edgingson its fore wings.

> ### ⑪ EATING AND DRINKING
> In the car park above the beach is the Chapel Porth Café, open every day from April to October and usually open weekends and school holidays from November until March. They serve hot and cold drinks breakfasts, lunch and snacks. The Victory Inn at Towan Cross has a good snacks menu and also does full meals. It's known for its good selection of real ales.

MINES AND METHODISM AT REDRUTH

A walk through Cornwall's mining heartland, visiting Methodism's famous outdoor 'cathedral' of Gwennap Pit.

The old Cornish town of Redruth gained its name from mineral mining. In medieval times, the process of separating tin and copper from waste materials turned a local river blood-red with washed out iron oxide. The innovative engineering that developed in tandem with mining, turned Redruth and Camborne into centres of Cornish industry.

Religious Zeal

Into the bleak world of 18th-century mineral mining came the brothers John and Charles Wesley, their religious zeal as hot as a Redruth furnace. It's very appropriate that one of the most revered locations in Methodism is Gwennap Pit, near Redruth. Here the grassy hollow of a caved-in mine shaft was first used for secular gatherings and events, which included cockfighting. But it wasn't long before the pit was commandeered as a venue for preaching. John Wesley preached here on 18 occasions between 1762 and 1789.

High Ground

The first part of this walk leads from Redruth past mining relics such as the great chimney stack of the Pednandrea Mine, just off Sea View Terrace. Once, the stack towered eight storeys high; it's now reduced to four, but is still impressive. From here you soon climb to the high ground of Gwennap and Carn Marth. The field path that takes you to Gwennap Pit was once a 'highway' of people heading for this 'cathedral of the moor'. Today there is a Visitor Centre at the Pit, alongside the peaceful little Busveal Chapel of 1836.

From Gwennap Pit the walk leads on to the summit of Carn Marth and to one of the finest viewpoints in Cornwall; unexpectedly so because of the hill's modest profile. From above the flooded quarry on the summit you look north to the sea and to the hill of St Agnes Beacon. North-east lies the St Austell clay country, south-west is the rocky summit of Carn Brea with its distinctive granite cross; south-east you can even see the cranes on Falmouth dockside. From the top of Carn Marth, the return route is all downhill along rough tracks and quiet country lanes that lead back to the heart of Redruth.

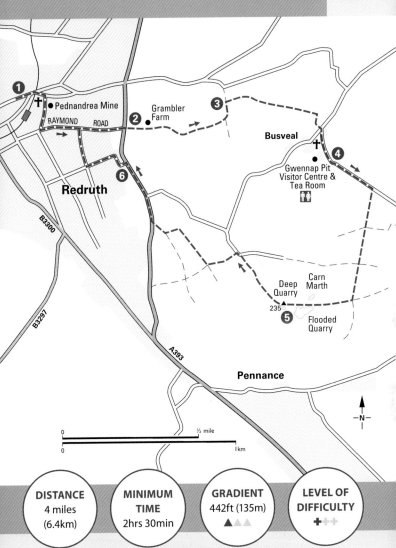

DISTANCE	MINIMUM TIME	GRADIENT	LEVEL OF DIFFICULTY
4 miles (6.4km)	2hrs 30min	442ft (135m) ▲▲▲	✚✚✚

PATHS Field paths, rough tracks and surfaced lanes. Can be muddy after rain, 6 stiles **LANDSCAPE** Small fields and open heathland with quarry and mine remains **SUGGESTED MAP** OS Explorer 104 Redruth & St Agnes **START/FINISH** Grid reference: SW 699421
DOG FRIENDLINESS Dogs on lead through grazed areas
PARKING Several car parks in Redruth
PUBLIC TOILETS Redruth car parks. Gwennap Pit Visitor Centre, when open

WALK 24 DIRECTIONS

❶ From any of the car parks, make your way to Fore Street. Walk up to a junction (the railway station is down to the right) and take the middle branch, to the left of the Wesley Centenary Memorial Building (now the YMCA) and signposted 'To Victoria Park'. This is Wesley Street. In just a few paces turn right on Sea View Terrace; the chimney stack of the Pednandrea Mine is up to the left a few paces along the road. Pass Basset Street on the right and, where streets cross, go left, all the way up Raymond Road to a T-junction with Sandy Lane.

❷ Cross the road with care, then follow the track opposite, signposted 'Public Bridleway' and 'Grambler Farm'. Go through a gate by the farm and continue to an open area. Bear left here and follow a track between hedges. At a junction with another track turn left, signposted 'Gwennap Pit'.

❸ Go right and over a stile next to a field gateway with breeze block gateposts. Cross a stile at the next gate then keep ahead across the next field. Cross a stile and continue between wire fences by a house to a final stile. Walk down a lane to a junction of roads and follow the road opposite for 100yds (91m) to Gwennap Pit.

❹ Follow the road away from Gwennap Pit. Ignore the first few turn offs and in about 300yds (274m)

turn off to the right along a track, signposted 'Public Bridleway'. Keep ahead at two crossings, then, at a final crossing beside a ruined building, turn right and up a stony track to the summit of Carn Marth.

❺ Pass a flooded quarry on your left, then follow a rocky path round right past a trig point and along the fenced-in rim of a quarry. Keep ahead at a junction and go down a track to reach a surfaced road. Turn left and in 30yds (27m) turn left along a track, signed 'Public Bridleway' to a T-junction with the main road at a house called Tara. Cross with care, turn right and continue for 300yds (274m).

> ⓌⓍ **EATING AND DRINKING**
> There is a tea room at the Gwennap Pit Visitor Centre. You can picnic in Gwennap Pit itself. Redruth has several restaurants, cafés and pubs to choose from. Sample the wonderful local Cornish pasties from WC Rowe's in Fore Street. The Red Lion pub is also in Fore Street, and there is a fish and chip shop in Green Lane.

❻ Go left at a junction, signposted as a cycle route, and follow a lane round right, then left into a broad avenue of houses. At a crossroads turn right along Trefusis Road. At the next junction turn left into Raymond Road and then turn right at the next crossroads into Sea View Terrace. Turn left down Wesley Street and on into Fore Street.

HIGH GROUND ON CARN BREA

A circuit of a wild and rocky hill above the urban sprawl.

Carn Brea is a big knuckly granite hill that rises to a height of 828ft (252m) above the mid-Cornwall towns of Camborne and Redruth. The industrial outskirts of the towns are landscapes of least beauty, as far as Cornwall goes. Tin and copper miners dug away at the low ground of this part of Cornwall for centuries. Railway and main roads cut through, and created unsympathetic strip development. Buildings spread out to the bleak edges of industrial estates. The towns almost merged and, as Cornish mining declined and Cornwall turned increasingly towards tourism and the 'invisible' service industries, Camborne and Redruth remained staunchly unglamorous and down to earth. Yet, the great hill of Carn Brea above the two towns survives as an iconic Cornish landscape.

You appreciate this best from the top of the hill. There are distant views of the sea and of the hills of St Agnes Beacon, Carn Marth and Carnkie and a landscape of villages, patchworked fields and woods; a countryside that is dotted with the ruins of mine engine houses and other buildings that have an almost medieval appearance. There is precedent for all this human settlement and development. Carn Brea was the site of a large neolithic encampment over 5,000 years ago.

Wind Polished

The summit of Carn Brea is studded with wind polished slabs and boulders of fantastical shapes. Granite extends the height of the hill by another 90ft (27m) thanks to the striking, if rather inelegant, Dunstanville Monument that crowns the flat summit ridge. It was built in 1837 in honour of local landowner, Sir Francis Basset, Lord Dunstanville, who profited hugely from local mining. On the eastern edge of the summit is the quirky Carn Brea Castle, entwined with a rock outcrop and now a restaurant of some character. A building of sorts has been recorded on this site since the 14th century and the original building was probably a hunting lodge or summerhouse of the Basset family. Such features are all part of the pleasure of Carn Brea for the walker – the modern world may be highly visible below, but ancient history is at your feet.

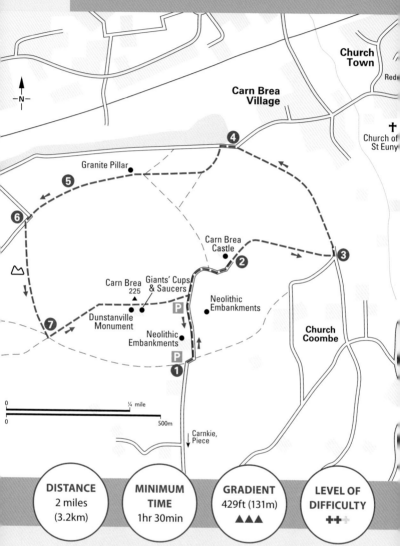

Church Town

Red

Carn Brea Village

Church of St Euny

4

Granite Pillar

5

6

Carn Brea Castle

2

3

Carn Brea 225 ▲

Giants' Cups & Saucers

Neolithic Embankments

Dunstanville Monument

Church Coombe

P

Neolithic Embankments

P

7

1

0 ¼ mile
0 500m

Carnkie, Piece

—N—

DISTANCE	MINIMUM TIME	GRADIENT	LEVEL OF DIFFICULTY
2 miles (3.2km)	1hr 30min	429ft (131m) ▲▲▲	✚✚✚

PATHS Rights of way and permissive paths; rocky in places. Wet and muddy on some sections **LANDSCAPE** A distinctive hill, covered in heath and studded with huge granite boulders **SUGGESTED MAP** OS Explorer 104 Redruth & St Agnes **START/FINISH** Grid reference: SW 685405 **DOG FRIENDLINESS** Some sections of route used by horse riders **PARKING** Small open area at end of narrow public road from Carnkie. Do not block gateway of a private house. A few parking spaces on hilltop along rough continuaton track from this parking area; park at your own risk **PUBLIC TOILETS** None on route

WALK 25 DIRECTIONS

❶ Walk up the rough stony track from the lower parking area and follow the track round right toward Carn Brea Castle. (If parking on the hilltop, follow the track to the castle.)

❷ Continue along the path that continues from a parking space beside the castle. Pass a granite slab and in about 20yds (18m) turn right and go down a path. Take the right-hand branch at a fork and continue downhill on a rocky path. The distinctive tower of St Euny's Church lies below.

❸ Turn left at a T-junction along a wide track. (Watch out for horse riders.)

❹ Turn left at a junction with a lane. In a few paces turn left along a narrow path beside a granite boulder. (The path ahead is stranded in places, but essentially follows the base of the hill slope.) Keep right at a fork. Keep left at the next fork and pass to the left of a granite pillar with bore holes in it.

❺ Reach a junction of paths. Follow the path directly opposite. Keep right at the next fork and then, in a few paces, keep straight across at a

> ### 🍴 EATING AND DRINKING
> The Countryman pub in the hamlet of Piece, just west of Carnkie village, does a good selection of sandwiches, baguettes and jacket potatoes as well as pub lunches and evening meals. Carn Brea Castle Restaurant is open in the evenings only and offers Mediterranean and Middle Eastern cuisine. Bookings only.

crossing of paths. Keep left at the next two junctions. Keep left of a raised area of ground. You are now abreast of a big granite outcrop on the hill above.

❻ Turn left at a T-junction in about 50yds (46m) and follow a steep, rocky and sometimes eroded path uphill. Pass the big granite outcrop that lies some distance to your left. Ignore a left-hand fork where the path levels off.

❼ In a few paces, reach a crossing of paths (there is a stone bench just to the right over a low bank). Turn left and follow a rocky path to the Dunstanville Monument and continue to the hilltop car parking areas. Turn right and follow the approach track downhill, if parked at the lower car park.

> ### 🔎 IN THE AREA
> A visit to the Church of St Euny, whose tower is visible from Point ❷ on the walk, is very worthwhile. St Euny's has a 19th-century Georgian main building which is grafted onto a 15th-century tower. St Euny's old graveyard surrounds the church and has fascinating headstones. The section among trees to the east is supremely Gothic in character.

COAST AND RIVER AT MAWNAN SMITH

A circular walk along the shores
of Helford's famous yachting haven.

The Helford River, known also as Helford Passage, represents Romantic Cornwall writ large. The quiet waters and deeply wooded banks inspire thoughts of tall sailing ships stealing in through dawn mist. The Helford is where the famous Cornish novelists, Sir Arthur Quiller-Couch and Daphne du Maurier set their romantic stories of Frenchman's Creek, a lonely inlet on the south shore of the river.

Perfect Hiding Place

Helford's cross-channel connections are historic. French privateers and smugglers, united with their Cornish brethren by what were once respected 'trades', must certainly have used the river as a perfect hiding place from storms and from the authorities. As late as the Second World War the Helford was used by the Special Operations Executive, which sent specially designed boats, disguised as Breton fishing vessels, to mingle with the French fishing fleet. They secretly passed on special agents, equipment and information under the eyes of a German-manned overseer vessel. Today the French connection is as strong as ever with countless cross-channel sailing trips to Brittany starting from The Helford.

Norman Building

The walk makes its pleasant way from Mawnan Church via inland footpaths to the coast and then round Toll Point overlooking the mouth of the river. The church is a handsome Norman building and the name Mawnan again underlines the area's strong connections with France as it is believed to have been the name of a Breton monk who settled here during the 6th century AD. The church stands on the site of a possible Bronze Age and Iron Age site, a typical progression in the siting of Cornish religious buildings. There are remnants of 13th-century constructions, not least the chancel of the church, where there is a fine piscina, a water basin, with carved heads as decoration. You can try out your Cornish language at the 19th-century lychgate whose inscription translates as 'It is good for me to draw nigh unto God'.

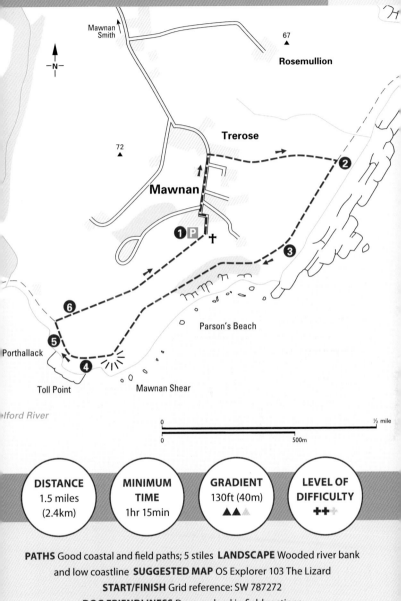

Mawnan Smith

67 ▲

Rosemullion

Mawnan Smith

—N—

72 ▲

Trerose

2

Mawnan

1 P ✝

3

Parson's Beach

6

5

Porthallack

4

Toll Point

Mawnan Shear

Iford River

0 ———————————— ½ mile

0 ———————————— 500m

DISTANCE
1.5 miles
(2.4km)

MINIMUM TIME
1hr 15min

GRADIENT
130ft (40m)
▲▲▲

LEVEL OF DIFFICULTY
✚✚✚

PATHS Good coastal and field paths; 5 stiles **LANDSCAPE** Wooded river bank
and low coastline **SUGGESTED MAP** OS Explorer 103 The Lizard
START/FINISH Grid reference: SW 787272
DOG FRIENDLINESS Dogs on lead in field sections
PARKING By Mawnan Church
PUBLIC TOILETS Opposite the Red Lion pub in Mawnan Smith village
(on road to Helford Passage)

WALK 26 DIRECTIONS

❶ Leave the car park and walk up the lane for about 300yds (274m). Just after a house, turn off right and follow a public footpath. Go over a stile and follow the left-hand edge of a field.

❷ Join the coast path at the bottom seaward corner of the field. Turn right and follow the coast path along the edge of the field and go over a wooden stile.

🦋 ON THE WALK

In spring and early summer the coastal footpath passes through a linear garden of wild flowers and plants such as vivid bluebells and the delicately sculpted early purple orchid.

🍴 EATING AND DRINKING

The attractive white-walled Red Lion pub in The Square at Mawnan Smith village does a selection of lunchtime dishes as well as sandwiches and soup. It also does evening meals and has a good selection of beers and other drinks.

---

❸ Continue along the coast path, descending steps into a wooded area. Go up more steps, emerge from the woods and go through a kissing gate into a field. Keep straight ahead along the field-edge, with views of the Helford River.

❹ Go through a kissing gate by a wooden bench and, immediately, go over a stone stile. Follow the path and soon descend some steps and continue along the river's edge.

❺ Go through a wooden gate into a field and keep straight ahead, descending steeply. Go through a kissing gate and at the small stony beach of Porthallack, turn right, just before a boathouse. Go through a kissing gate and follow a signposted public footpath.

❻ Follow the well-defined path along field-edges crossing two stiles on the way (dogs on lead here). After the second stile keep ahead and uphill to reach a wooden gate into the car park.

🌀 IN THE AREA

A visit to the nearby National Trust Glendurgan Garden is an absolute must. The garden is about 0.25 mile (400m) south-west of Mawnan Smith on the road to the village of Durgan. This lovely garden, in its almost sub-tropical valley, was established in the 1820s and 1830s by the Quaker industrialist Alfred Fox. The garden contains a wealth of trees and exotic plants including New Zealand tree ferns, while familiar species include azaleas, hydrangeas and camellias. There is an entertaining maze for all the family to enjoy.

HIDDEN CORNERS AT PORTHALLOW

Get away from it all along the coast path
and through peaceful fields at Porthallow.

The coastline that runs south from the estuary of the Helford River to Porthallow is uncrowded and serene, although the sea can soon whip up a storm along its rocky shoreline, when it's in the mood. At Porthallow, and further south again at Porthoustocks there is a striking contrast with the picturesque Helford, however. Here the Cornish coast has been sacrificed to full-scale quarrying that has left a wrenched landscape in its wake. Porthoustock Quarry is still raw and desolate from ongoing activity, but, at Porthallow, the quarry has been out of use for some time and is now muffled by a green cloak of vegetation and softened by the presence of the sea.

Pilchard Boats

Porthallow, or 'Pralla' as it is known locally, was a busy pilchard fishing village during the 19th century and into the first decade of the 20th century, until the shoals dwindled. In those days there would have been a number of pilchard boats stationed here, ready to launch when shoals were spotted. The boats fed out large seine nets round the shoals and then steadily drew in the ends of the net to 'bag' the fish. There are still a few old pilchard cellars behind the beach at Porthallow where the pilchards were pressed for oil. The fish were then packed tightly into barrels between layers of salt for export to Catholic Italy, mainly to satisfy the high demands for fish during the Lenten period.

Manacles Reef

Today at Porthallow there is a wide stony beach, which was created from quarry waste. Some fishing boats still work from the beach and Porthallow is a favourite launching site for diving boats that take divers out to the area of the notorious Manacles reef, a mile (1.6km) or so to the south, and a graveyard of numerous vessels over the centuries. Your walk takes you north from Pralla through a bracing coastal landscape and then wanders inland across fields and along old farm tracks to the tiny settlement at Roskorwell. Here, diligent care of verges and a central grassy area has created a little 'village green' that is entirely rural and detached from the emphatic sea-girt spirit of Pralla below.

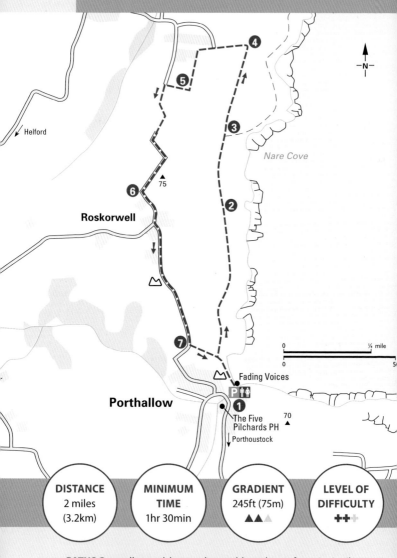

Helford

4

5

3

Nare Cove

75

6

Roskorwell

2

0   ¼ mile
0   5

7

Fading Voices

P

Porthallow

1

The Five
Pilchards PH

70

Porthoustock

DISTANCE	MINIMUM TIME	GRADIENT	LEVEL OF DIFFICULTY
2 miles (3.2km)	1hr 30min	245ft (75m) ▲▲▲	✚✚✚

PATHS Generally good, but can be muddy and wet after rain; 2 stiles
LANDSCAPE Low rocky coastline backed by gently sloping fields
SUGGESTED MAP OS Explorer 103 The Lizard
START/FINISH Grid reference: SW 798232
DOG FRIENDLINESS Dogs should be kept under strict control
through field sections **PARKING** Porthallow Beach
PUBLIC TOILETS Porthallow

WALK 27 DIRECTIONS

❶ Leave by the car park entrance and turn right, signposted 'Coast Path'. Climb steep steps (handrail) past a house and continue along a path between hedges. At a junction where stone steps go up left, keep along the coast path. Keep right at the next fork.

❷ Keep right at a fork and follow the coast path. Go over a stile into a field by a National Trust sign for Nare Point. Keep ahead across the field toward bushes, where there is a signpost.

❸ Bear right to the cliff-edge side of the field. Leave the coast path just before a stile and go up the right-hand edge of the field.

❹ Exit the field at its top right-hand corner and go up a track towards an isolated house. Go alongside the house's garden wall, turn left round an open metal gate then through a gate into a field. Follow the right edge of the field uphill (this section is a legally diverted right of way).

❺ Turn right at the top corner of the field and along a grassy track, bearing round left and into a field. Head diagonally right across the middle of the field to its top edge and then turn right along the field edge to a white gate in the field corner. Go through the gate and follow a hedged-in path.

> ### ⚓ ON THE WALK
> Porthallow is the half-way mark in the South West Coast Path, the National Trail that runs for 630 miles (1,014km) from Minehead in Somerset to Poole in Dorset. To celebrate the fact there is distinctive sculpture called 'Fading Voices' at the entrance to Porthallow beach.

❻ Keep along a farm track and pass a cottage on your right. Continue to the public road at Roskorwell with its neatly trimmed verges. Keep straight across and go down the narrow lane opposite.

❼ Where the lane bends to the right, go left and over a stile, signposted 'Porthallow', and straight down the field past telegraph poles. Go through a hedged-in section then down some steps to a junction with the coast path. Turn right to the car park at Porthallow.

🍴 EATING AND DRINKING
It seems fitting that Porthallow's pub should be called The Five Pilchards and in keeping with the nautical theme the pub is full of local artefacts and relics from the many ships wrecked off the coast here. There's a good selection of drinks including some fine Cornish ales. They do pub lunches and evening meals and the fish, not surprisingly, is a specialty.

ART ALONG THE COVERACK COAST

An intriguing walk along the coast path leads inland
to a remarkable sculpture garden.

Coverack may seem well protected from Cornwall's great westerly storms
by its east-facing location and by the protective bulwarks of both Lizard
Head and the nearby Black Head. This can be a stormy place, however, and
an enduring reminder of this is the name of the village's famous Paris Hotel,
named after a ship that was wrecked here in 1899. Coverack is still a favoured
place and is hugely popular with beach-loving families and with windsurfers.

Pilchard Fishing

The village's strong identity was forged in medieval times when Coverack was
a thriving pilchard fishing port. Its modern name derives from the medieval
name Porthcovrek, one meaning of which is 'the cove (Porth) of the stream'.
Fishing continued from Coverack throughout the centuries but declined from
the early 20th century onwards when the pilchard shoals declined. This could
have been because of overfishing, but also because of the behaviour of fish
species that seem to abandon once favoured waters without reason. Fishing
boats still work from Coverack's tiny harbour, and just beyond the harbour
this walk begins at Dolor Point, the far seaward end of the village.

Rugged Cliff

You head south from Dolor Point through the outskirts of Coverack, but soon
reach the coast path and Chynhalls Point, a narrow rocky headland. An Iron
Age promontory settlement is thought to have been sited here. Below is
Porthbeer Cove with its wide apron of flat, sea-stained rock and with an outer
area of sand that is covered at high tide. The steep slopes that rise above
Porthbeer are fascinating. Part of the path you follow crosses areas of wet
'flushes' where springs and watercourses create permanently damp swathes
of vegetation. Beyond here the path winds steeply uphill through rocky steps
to the flat cliff top. The return route to Coverack passes the wonderful Terence
Coventry sculpture garden. Thereafter the final stroll back to Coverack is
untaxing and once again draws a sharp contrast between the rawness of the
wild coastline and the picturesque village.

Opposite: A picturesque thatched cottage in Coverack

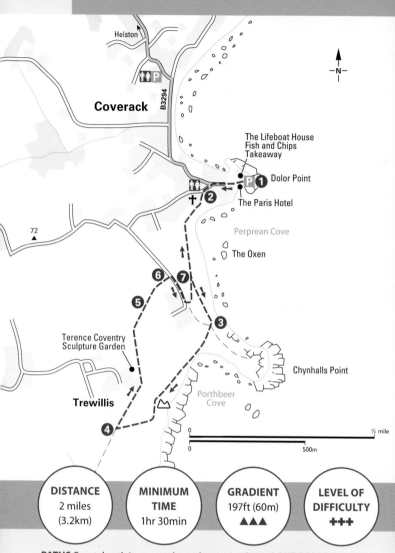

DISTANCE
2 miles
(3.2km)

MINIMUM TIME
1hr 30min

GRADIENT
197ft (60m)
▲▲▲

LEVEL OF DIFFICULTY
+++

PATHS Coastal path is very rocky and steep in places **LANDSCAPE** A complex coastal area of rocky pinnacles and wooded hinterland
SUGGESTED MAP OS Explorer 103 The Lizard **START/FINISH** Grid reference: SW 786182 **DOG FRIENDLINESS** Off lead but under control near houses
PARKING Small car park at Dolor Point or a public car park at the entrance to Coverack, coming from Helston on the B3294 **PUBLIC TOILETS** By main car park and before The Paris Hotel **NOTE** If parking at the main car park, you need to walk through Coverack to the start. There and back is an additional 0.5 miles (800m)

WALK 28 DIRECTIONS

❶ Join the coastal footpath at the inner corner of the car park and follow the path above a rocky beach. Pass behind a house and go right, up steep stone steps. Follow the path past several benchs to reach the public road.

❷ Turn left and, in a few paces, leave the road, and go straight ahead along a surfaced path to the left of an old Wesleyan Chapel. Pass in front of a row of cottages. At a junction take the left-hand path, signposted 'Coast Path'. Keep left at a junction, by a stone bench and reach a junction of several paths at Chynhalls Point.

❸ Take the second path on the left (the first path on the left leads out to Chynhalls Point). Descend to a grassy area from where a path leads down to the beach in Porthbeer Cove. Follow the coast path crossing wetland areas by a wooden bridge and boardwalk sections. The path steepens and becomes very rocky.

❹ At a junction of paths, where the ground levels off, go right. Pass through a wide grassy area with rocky pinnacles to seaward. Reach the Terence Coventry Sculpture Park. On the main route continue along the path, cross a small field and go through a gapway (stone stile on its left).

❺ Enter woodland, cross a small stream by easy stepping stones and continue through the woods on a broad track. The track becomes a path that leads between hedges and past the edge of a caravan park. Follow a grassy track leading alongside the garden wall of a large bungalow.

❻ Reach a surfaced road. (Dogs should be kept on lead by houses.) Turn right and walk past some houses. At the entrance to a large building, go left across the road and down a path, descending steps to reach a T-junction. Turn left and follow the path downhill to reach a junction beside the stone bench described earlier.

❼ Keep left and retrace the first section of the walk to the car park.

A GODREVY WALKABOUT

A stroll around Godrevy Point with views
of the lighthouse that inspired Virginia Woolf.

Godrevy is seal watching country and it's worth taking binoculars with you, for spotting seabirds as well. The headland stands at the northern end of a long swathe of golden sand that runs for 3 miles (4.8km) from the mouth of the Hayle River and marks the eastern arm of St Ives Bay.

Inspiring Place

Godrevy is an inspiring place, not least for the dramatic lighthouse that lies offshore on the rocky Godrevy Island. The lighthouse serves to warn shipping of the long reef called The Stones that extends out to sea for over 2 miles (3.2km). Today the lighthouse is automated and no lighthouse-keepers occupy the tall handsome building or cultivate the kitchen garden within its walled compound. Godrevy Light inspired the novelist Virginia Woolf who spent many family holidays in St Ives. The headland is made up of two blunt-faced promontories, which are backed by sweeping grassland. The National Trust owns most of the headland today.

Grey Seals

There are very high cliffs at Godrevy, a dramatic contrast to the wide sweep of sand that lies due south and projects for nearly 0.5 miles (800m) inland at Gwithian. The cliffs are very high along the eastern edge of the headland, bordering an area known as The Knavocks. A subsidiary headland here is called Navax Point, yet another bewildering, yet endearing contradiction in coastal nomenclature. A high point of this walk is the possibility of spotting large numbers of grey seals hauled out at the base of the headland's cliffs especially at Mutton Cove, just east of Godrevy Point, the headland directly opposite Godrevy Island. The grey seal is Britain's commonest. At one time seals happily gathered, bred and gave birth to their pups on beaches that are now major tourist draws, and over the years these fascinating creatures have retreated to sea caves and rocky islands. They still haul out on inaccessible shores, however, and Godrevy is a favourite haven for them and they should not be disturbed or harassed.

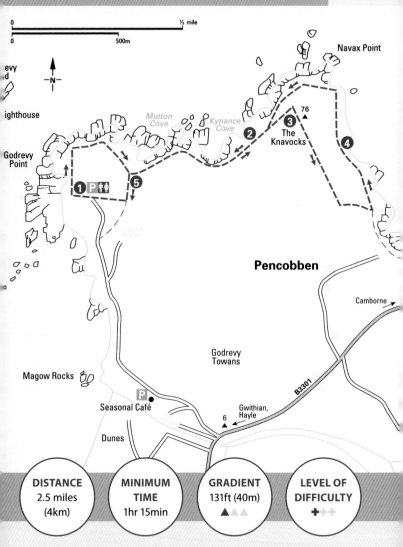

DISTANCE
2.5 miles
(4km)

MINIMUM TIME
1hr 15min

GRADIENT
131ft (40m)
▲▲▲

LEVEL OF DIFFICULTY
✚✚✚

PATHS Mainly level and well-defined. Can be muddy during wet weather
LANDSCAPE Airy headland of grassy heathland ringed by steep cliffs
SUGGESTED MAP OS Explorer 102 Land's End
START/FINISH Grid reference: SW 582431
DOG FRIENDLINESS Under control due to possible livestock grazing
PARKING National Trust higher car park. There is a lower car park by the seasonal café **PUBLIC TOILETS** By approach to higher car park (seasonal)

WALK 29 DIRECTIONS

❶ Join the coastal footpath at the seaward edge of the car park and go right. Go over a stile and keep straight ahead on the main path. Keep right at a fork in 50yds (46m). Follow a well-defined path that eventually leads along the edge of the cliff.

❷ Go through a gate and into a field. In about 50yds (46m) leave the main path and follow a grassy path diagonally right across the field.

❸ Just before a trig point, take a narrow path to the right and keep straight ahead where the path widens. Join a grassy track and turn left. A few paces before a gate take the narrow path leading off to the left of the gate. Reach a wooden stile. Do not cross the stile; instead, turn left along the coast path.

❹ Follow the stony path round the headland of The Knavocks. Continue across a field and go through the gate previously met at Point **❷**. Retrace your outgoing route along the cliff top.

❺ Reach a fenced section of the cliff edge and in a few paces turn left down a grassy track to return to the car park.

> ### ⌀ IN THE AREA
> In Gwithian village is the rather splendidly named Church of St Gocianus. Gwithian was probably an important religious site from the early days of the Celtic 'Saints' and there was an oratory on the sands said to date from those times. The church is mainly 19th century but the lych gate has 15th-century elements.

> ### 🛈 EATING AND DRINKING
> There is a seasonal café at the first National Trust car park that you come to as you drive up to the Godrevy higher car park. They offer excellent snacks, cakes and hot and cold drinks. At the nearby village of Gwithian is The Red River pub, previously the Pendarves Arms, where they do pub lunches and meals and have a good selection of real ales.

> ### ⚓ ON THE WALK
> The skies offshore from Godrevy are often full of seabirds. These may include cormorant, fulmar, guillemot and razorbills. Look out for the gannet, a magnificent bird that can have a wingspan of over 6ft (2m). The gannet has an imperious head with black eye markings and a light yellow poll. It has a very strong beak and no external nostrils while its head is further protected by air sacs. This is all useful for its method of catching fish, a spectacular plunge from on high into the sea, its wings half-folded like a trident.

Opposite: Sea stacks on Gwithian Beach

WOODS AND WATER AT THE LOE

A walk beside The Loe, a one-time river estuary turned into a seashore lake.

The sea rarely loses out to the land, but this walk takes you round an inland lake that was once an estuary of the sea. Today, the sea may grumble in the distance, but the quiet lake waters of The Loe lie peacefully within wooded environs below the ancient Cornish town of Helston and are a haven for birds.

Stannary Town

Helston flourished during Cornwall's historic tin and copper mining era when it was a designated 'Stannary' town. This meant that the town held rights of measuring and assaying tin and so profited from it. But Helston originated many years before this period when it was a seagoing port on the then estuary of the River Cober. Success from mining brought its own penalties as sediments brought down by the river from tin processing deep inland built up across the mouth of the Cober and eventually turned Helston into an inland town. Tidal movements added to the build up of materials so that, eventually, a barrier spanned the mouth of the estuary trapping an expanse of water behind it. This stretch of water became the famous Loe Pool, called more accurately The Loe, from the Cornish word 'logh' for pool.

Wetland Environment

The same process of silt deposit has seen the head of The Loe develop into a classic wetland environment while the great expanse of water lying between this and the bar is one of the finest wildfowl overwintering sites in Cornwall. Even such a rare visitor as the osprey has been recorded here. The commonest birds likely to be seen as you walk along the wooded shoreline during the first part of the walk are coot, widgeon, mallard and teal. You might even see a cormorant on an inland foray and herons roost in the tall pines on the west side of The Loe near Loe Bar. The Loe was once part of the Penrose Estate, an ownership that dates from the 13th century until it came into the hands of the Rogers family during the 1770s. Extensive landscaping and woodland planting by the Rogers has resulted in today's park-like aspect of The Loe area and today the estate is in the care of the National Trust.

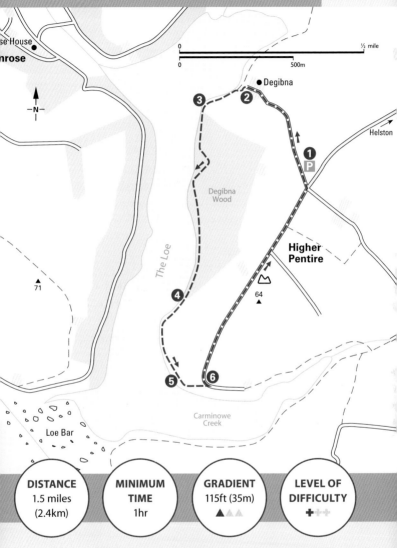

se House
nrose

—N—

½ mile

0
500m

• Degibna

3

2

Helston

1
P

Degibna
Wood

The Loe

**Higher
Pentire**

71

64

4

5

6

Carminowe
Creek

Loe Bar

DISTANCE	MINIMUM TIME	GRADIENT	LEVEL OF DIFFICULTY
1.5 miles (2.4km)	1hr	115ft (35m) ▲▲▲	+++

PATHS Farm tracks, woodland and field paths
LANDSCAPE A gentle countryside of woods and lakeside habitats with the sea in
the background **SUGGESTED MAP** OS Explorer 103 The Lizard
START/FINISH Grid reference: SW 653252 **DOG FRIENDLINESS** On lead
throughout field sections and areas where stock might be grazed
PARKING National Trust car park (free) at the end of Degibna Lane (access lane
near junction of A394 and A3083 **PUBLIC TOILETS** Helston

WALK 30 DIRECTIONS

❶ Walk down the concreted lane leading off through a gapway from the far end of the car park. A few paces into the walk you catch a first passing glimpse of the shining surface of The Loe in the valley below, with Penrose House beyond.

❷ Where the lane ends at Degibna, bear down left between buildings, go through a stagger gate and then follow a stony path downhill into deep woodland and past a small stone barn. At a junction by the water's edge, turn left, signposted 'Loe Bar'.

❸ Go through a wooden kissing gate and follow a permissive path along the edge of The Loe. Ascend some steps and go right at a junction. Keep right at the next junction. At the next junction keep straight ahead and downhill.

❹ Go through a wooden kissing gate where the wood ends and follow a faint field path alongside the water.

> 🍴 **EATING AND DRINKING**
> There are no refreshment points on route, but the grassy areas beyond Degibna Wood, or the beach at Loe Bar make for lovely picnic spots. Helston has a number of cafés and pubs.

❺ Follow the path round the edge of the subsidiary Carminowe Creek. Go through a wooden kissing gate and through a stand of hawthorns to a junction with a wide track.

❻ Turn left and follow the track uphill to return to the car park. You can, if you choose, extend your route (see In the Area panel below).

> 🐾 **ON THE WALK**
> The ubiquitous grey squirrel lords it over Degibna Wood, and with some insouciance, to say the least. You may even find a baby squirrel or two investigating you at close quarters. They have been known to perch on the toes of walkers' boots and even run up a trouser leg or two.

> 🧭 **IN THE AREA**
> You can extend your route to visit Loe Bar by following the track to the right at Point ❻. This will lead to a boardwalk crossing of the head of Carminowe Creek. Turn right here and follow the south edge of Carminowe Creek to reach Loe Bar. It is very dangerous to enter the water anywhere from Loe Bar and from the beach leading north-west to Porthleven. There are strong currents, unpredictable swells and a deadly undertow. You need to retrace your steps to rejoin the main walk.

THE SERPENTINE ROUTE TO CADGWITH

A walk between land and sea through the serpentine landscape of the Lizard peninsula.

The serpentine rock of the Lizard Peninsula is fascinating by name and by nature. The name derives from the sinuous veins of green, red, yellow and white that wriggle across the dark green or brownish-red surface of the rock. The best quality serpentine is easily carved and shaped and can be polished to a sheen. You can admire this quality on this walk, especially where stiles are built of serpentine slabs; their surfaces are mirror-smooth and slippery from use. Admire, but take care when climbing over them when they are wet.

Height of Fashion

In the 19th century serpentine furnishings were the height of fashion and the material was used for shopfronts and fireplaces. The industry declined during the 1890s however and cheaper, more resilient marble from Italy and Spain began to dominate the market. Today serpentine craftsmen still operate in little workshops on the Lizard and you can buy serpentine souvenirs at Lizard village. At Carleon Cove, half-way through the walk, you'll find the ruins of waterwheels, steam engines, machine shops, storehouses and a factory where serpentine was processed until the early 1890s. Today Carleon Cove is in the care of the National Trust.

Landslip

From Carleon Cove the walk leads along a fascinating section of coast. At Enys Head there is a vast gulf in the cliff where a landslip occurred in the distant past and further on at Kildown Point is the old Signal Staff Quarry, which supplied the Poltesco serpentine works with raw material. Kildown Point itself was for long known locally as The Beacon due to its use as a site for sending signals. As you approach Cadgwith you pass a strange little building with a tall chimney. This dates from the beginning of the 19th century when local coastguards established it as a watch house. Cadgwith is an archetypal Cornish fishing village where fishing boats are launched from the shingle beach. Much of the village's charm comes from its thatched cottages, a rare sight in windy Cornwall.

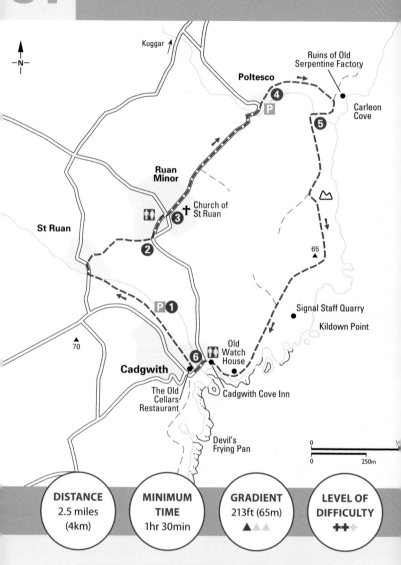

DISTANCE
2.5 miles (4km)

MINIMUM TIME
1hr 30min

GRADIENT
213ft (65m)
▲▲▲

LEVEL OF DIFFICULTY
✚✚✚

PATHS Very good. Occasionally rocky on parts of coast section. Rocks can be slippery when wet **LANDSCAPE** Landlocked lanes and woodland tracks, coastal footpaths; 8 stiles **SUGGESTED MAP** OS Explorer 103 The Lizard **START/FINISH** Grid reference: SW 719147
DOG FRIENDLINESS Please keep under control in built-up areas
PARKING Cadgwith car park. About 0.25 miles (400m) inland from the village. Can be very busy in summer **PUBLIC TOILETS** Ruan Minor and Cadgwith

WALK 31 DIRECTIONS

❶ Go left along a grassy ride below the car park, to a stile. Continue through a gate and into woodland. Cross a stile into a public lane and turn right.

❷ Where the lane bends to the left turn off and go up a track on the right. In about 20yds (18m) take the first track on the right. This narrows to a path. Cross two stiles and finally go up stone steps to reach the main road at Ruan Minor. Go left and, just beyond the shop, turn left down a path by a signpost.

❸ Rejoin the main road by a thatched cottage (there are toilets just before the road). Cross diagonally right, and then go down a lane next to a school, passing the Church of St Ruan. In about

500yds (457m), just past an old mill and a bridge, go right at a T-junction to reach the car park at Poltesco.

❹ At the far end of the car park go through a gate and follow a track, signposted 'Carleon Cove'. Go right at a junction.

> **⚘ ON THE WALK**
> In the valley leading down from Poltesco to Carleon Cove you may spot Babington's leek, a plant that can reach 5ft (1.5m) in height. On the coast proper look for the sturdy tree mallow, a tall plant with a hairy stem and purple flowers.

> **⚲ IN THE AREA**
> The Church of St Ruan is a small, endearing building built mainly of local serpentine stone. It has a low tower, as if bitten off by the notorious Lizard wind. The east window is dedicated to Thomas Richard Collinson Harrison, a 16 year old who died in a cliff fall in 1909.

❺ Cross a wooden bridge above the cove, then climb steps and turn left at a T-junction. Turn left again in 0.25 miles (400m) where the path branches. Go through a kissing gate and continue along the cliff-edge path crossing stiles. Take care near the cliff edge.

❻ At Cadgwith turn left along the road behind the beach. Just beyond the public toilets, go right and up a signposted path between thatched cottages. Follow the path uphill to reach a stile and the car park.

> **🍴 EATING AND DRINKING**
> The Cadgwith Cove Inn at Cadgwith has a good selection of pub food including some tasty crab soup and fresh mussels as well as pasties, baguettes and pizzas. The Old Cellars Restaurant in Cadgwith is licensed and features the courtyard of an old pilchard processing 'cellars' right opposite Cadgwith harbour beach. Morning coffee, lunch, afternoon tea with tasty home-made cakes, and evening meals.

ST IVES TOWN AND COUNTRY

A contrasting walk through the streets of St Ives
and then along a rugged coast.

You have to share St Ives with many other people, but even in high season
this famous Cornish town can charm anyone and you can soon escape the
crowds by following this pleasant walk along the western shore. But, first,
you start at the very heart of St Ives, alongside a great open sweep of sandy
harbour that seems to trap all the light ever needed by the myriad of artists
who have been inspired by this enchanting place for well over a century.

The Island

The walk takes you along the bustling harbourside and past St Ives' excellent
local museum where good old-fashioned curatorship has resulted in an
Aladdin's Cave of fascinating artefacts. It's certainly worth a visit. Beyond here
you pass above the attractive little Porthgwidden Beach and up and over the
town's conspicuous headland known as The Island. On top of The Island are a
National Coastwatch Institution lookout and the little Chapel of St Nicholas.
The chapel dates from the 16th century when it was used, not only as a
seaman's chapel but also as an early form of lighthouse. In later years revenue
men on the watch for smugglers used it as a lookout. Below here to the
west is the magnificent Porthmeor Beach, one of Cornwall's premier surfing
beaches. It is also ideal for sunbathing, and for swimming, provided you pay
heed to safety flags and lifeguards. Above the beach stands the famous Tate
St Ives Gallery, celebrating the work of mainly Modern artists from St Ives.

Open Coast

Beyond all this, the crowds thin out dramatically and within minutes you are
on the open coast heading west. On this coastal footpath and the inland field
paths that follow, you tread in the footsteps of smugglers and revenue men,
Victorian coastguards and Godfearing Cornish folk. The second part of the
walk leads you inland along broad tracks between the high granite walls,
known as 'hedges' in Cornwall. Soon you feel as if you've lost the sea but
the way leads along field paths and across a sequence of granite stiles back
towards St Ives, to the great surf at Porthmeor and to the Tate St Ives Gallery.

Opposite: Fishing boats in the harbour at St Ives

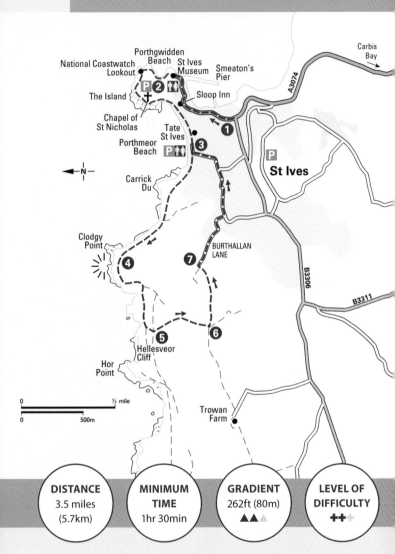

DISTANCE	MINIMUM TIME	GRADIENT	LEVEL OF DIFFICULTY
3.5 miles (5.7km)	1hr 30min	262ft (80m) ▲▲▲	++✛

PATHS Coastal path can be quite rocky. Field paths are good but can be very wet; 5 stiles **LANDSCAPE** Urban streets, a very scenic section of coast and small inland fields **SUGGESTED MAP** OS Explorer 102 Land's End **START/FINISH** Grid reference: SW 521408 **DOG FRIENDLINESS** Dogs under strict control through field areas. See note on dog ban at Point ❷ **PARKING** The Island car park, St Ives or other car parks **PUBLIC TOILETS** Smeaton's Pier, Porthgwidden Beach and Porthmeor Beach car park

WALK 32 DIRECTIONS

❶ Walk along the harbourfront towards Smeaton's Pier. Just before the pier entrance, turn left, signed to 'St Ives Museum'. Where the road bends, keep straight on into Wheal Dream. Turn right past St Ives Museum, then follow a walkway to Porthgwidden Beach.

❷ Cross the car park above the beach and climb to the National Coastwatch Institution lookout. Go down steps, behind the building at the back of the lookout, and then follow a footway to Porthmeor Beach. Go along the beach. (Half-way along the beach a ramp and steps lead up to the Tate Gallery St Ives.) At the beach end, go up to the car park. Note: There is a dog ban during the day on Porthmeor Beach from about Easter to the end of September. If you are walking with a dog you will need to go inland from the beach and walk along back Road West and then Porthmeor Road to the car park.

❸ Go up steps beside the public toilets, then turn right along a surfaced track past bowling and putting greens. Continue to the rocky headlands of Carrick Du and Clodgy Point.

❹ Walk uphill from Clodgy Point and follow the path round to the right. Continue along a very rocky path. In about 0.5 miles (800m) go left at a junction by a big boulder smothered with yellow lichen.

❺ At a T-junction with a track just past a National Trust sign, 'Hellesveor Cliff', turn left. Reach a track and turn left to follow the track between high walls. Go through a metal gate and reach a bend with stone stiles to either side.

❻ Go over the left-hand stile and follow a well-defined path through trees. Go over a stile and keep to the left-edges of small fields. Pass a field gap on the left and turn left just before a rusty gate. Follow a path between bushes and go through a small gate.

❼ Go over a stile into a field, bear round left and over another stile. Continue between high hedges to a stile into a surfaced lane. Turn right (Burthallan Lane). Turn left at a junction with a road. Follow the road to walk downhill and round left and down a steep hill. Keep round right to Porthmeor Beach and the Tate St Ives Gallery. Retrace your steps to the start.

---

⑪ EATING AND DRINKING

There are no refreshment points once you leave St Ives, but the town has numerous pubs, restaurants and takeaways. The Sloop Inn, mid-way along the harbourfront, is a famous harbourside inn that does pub food and is usually very busy. There are several other restaurants, cafés and fast food outlets along the harbourfront.

ON TOP OF THE WORLD AT TRENCROM

An Iron Age hilltop site
with spectacular views.

The 550ft (168m) Trencrom Hill is clearly visible from the A30 as you drive onto the Land's End Peninsula. It stands out against a smooth backdrop of higher ground, a distinctive beehive of a hill. It was this strategic position that made Trencrom the ideal venue for a prehistoric 'castle' and the flat summit of the hill once contained a small Iron Age settlement at this gateway to the 'First and Last' outpost of ancient Britain.

Wildlife Habitat

Today Trencrom is in the care of the National Trust and is a splendid wildlife habitat. There is a pleasant feeling of being marooned deep inland at the start of this walk as you pass through a tunnel of blackthorn and hawthorn trees, wreathed in ivy. Soon, you emerge into a more open landscape of dense vegetation, dwarf oak and sycamore trees. Look out for the small perching birds, known as passerines, such as stonechat and yellowhammer and listen for their brisk chirping. The plant life of this lush, damp habitat includes willowherb, yarrow, betony and the common mouse-ear with tiny white petals.

Sweeping Views

As you reach the top of the hill you pass between two granite uprights. These are the 'doorposts' of an overgrown embankment that still encircles the summit of the hill and is believed to date from at least the early Iron Age. Several hollows on the summit itself indicate the sites of possible Iron Age stone huts. The strategic importance that the site must have had at the time is clear. There are sweeping views to the east, and towards the thickening waist of Cornwall, from where enemies might well have come. To the north east lies the half moon of St Ives Bay. To the south is the vast open gulf of Mount's Bay with its rocky island of St Michael's Mount. Immediately west and north of Trencrom the view is more immediately of small compact fields, dotted with clumps of trees and farm settlements, all in rich greens and browns. Enjoy this glorious panorama as you turn full circle on the walk route.

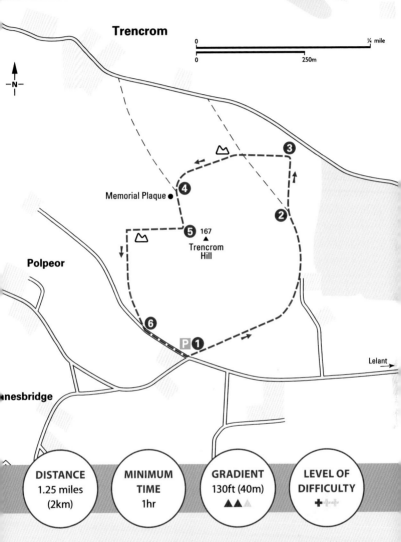

Trencrom

250m
¼ mile

—N—

Memorial Plaque ●

3

4

2

5 167
▲ Trencrom Hill

Polpeor

6

P **1**

Lelant

nesbridge

DISTANCE 1.25 miles (2km)	MINIMUM TIME 1hr	GRADIENT 130ft (40m) ▲▲△	LEVEL OF DIFFICULTY ✚✚✚

PATHS Very good and well-defined, but are narrow in places; can be muddy in wet weather **LANDSCAPE** Grassy hill dotted with trees and granite outcrops **SUGGESTED MAP** OS Explorer 102 Land's End **START/FINISH** Grid reference: SW 518359 **DOG FRIENDLINESS** Dogs can be let off lead, but should be kept within control, as horse riders are frequent users of the lower paths and lanes **PARKING** Small National Trust car park (free) on the south side of the hill **PUBLIC TOILETS** None on route

WALK 33 DIRECTIONS

1 Go through a metal gate to the left of the car park entrance, facing out. Follow the path alongside trees and shrubs and past a cottage on the right.

2 At a junction keep to the right-hand path. Go through a wooden barrier and reach a cross-junction.

3 Turn left and climb steadily uphill. Keep straight on at a junction. Soon you rise above the tree line and superb views of the sea open to the north east with a focal point being the offshore Godrevy Lighthouse.

4 Pass between a tall granite pillar on your right and a shorter pillar on the left to reach the flat grassy summit of Trencrom Hill.

5 Walk straight ahead past a flat rock and when you are abreast of two more flat rocks on the left, bear sharp left and follow a grassy path downhill.

6 On reaching a T-junction with a broad track, turn left along the track to return to the car park.

🍴 EATING AND DRINKING

There is no finer spot for a picnic than the top of Trencrom Hill, provided the wind is not in boisterous mood. Otherwise The Tyringham Arms is located just to the north of the hill. It is best reached by driving east from the car park and then turning left at a junction and keeping right at the immediate next junction.

⚓ ON THE WALK

When you reach the summit of Trencrom Hill explore the granite outcrop on your right. On its far side is a faded plaque fixed to the rock. This records the gift of Trencrom Hill to the National Trust by a local landowner, Lt Col Tyringnam of the Trevethoe Estate, in 1946. The sole condition of the gift was that the hill should stand forever as a memorial to the Cornish dead of the 20th century's two world wars.

🏛 IN THE AREA

Just down the road to the east of Trencrom Hill is another granite edifice, the handsome Lelant Church of St Uny perched in a lovely setting above the sandy Hayle Estuary. The present church is Norman in origin but all that remains of that time, among later additions and refurbishments, are two Romanesque piers supporting a Norman arch. The church was once the focus of a medieval settlement and was twice buried by drifting sands during the medieval period.

THE SMUGGLER KING OF PRUSSIA COVE

An exhilarating coastal walk through the domain of one of Cornwall's most famous smugglers.

Smuggling clings to the image of Cornwall like the Atlantic mist through which the old time 'freetraders' so often stole ashore with their cargoes of tea, spirits, tobacco, silk, china and even playing cards.

Mount's Bay

Such 'honest adventuring' seems personified by the famous Carter family who lived at Prussia Cove on the eastern shores of Mount's Bay in West Cornwall. The cove is really more of a series of rocky inlets close to the magnificent St Michael's Mount, the castle-crowned island that so enhances the inner corner of Mount's Bay. John and Henry (Harry) Carter were the best-known members of the family and ran their late 18th-century smuggling enterprise with great flair and efficiency. They even fortified the headland overlooking Prussia Cove in a move that echoed the defensive settlements of the Celtic Iron Age. John Carter was the more flamboyant, styling himself in early childhood games as 'the King of Prussia' an indication of contemporary awareness of the activities of Fredrick the Great of Prussia. The name stuck and the original Porth Leah Cove became known as the 'King of Prussia's Cove'. Fame indeed. John Carter had integrity. He once broke in to an excise store in Penzance to recover smuggled goods confiscated from Prussia Cove in his absence. The authorities knew it must have been Carter because they said he was 'an upright man' and took only his own goods. His brother Harry became a Methodist preacher and forbade swearing on all his vessels.

The remote Prussia Cove says everything about the environment within which smuggling flourished. As you follow the route of the walk inland, you can sense the remoteness of hamlet and cottage still, the secretiveness of the lanes and paths that wriggle inland from a coast that is formidable, yet accessible to skilled seamen. At Perranuthnoe, the narrow, flat beach resounds with the sound of the sea where modern surfers and holidaymakers now enjoy themselves. From here the coastal footpath leads back along the coast across the rocky headland of Cudden Point to where a series of secluded coves make up the Carter's old kingdom of Prussia Cove.

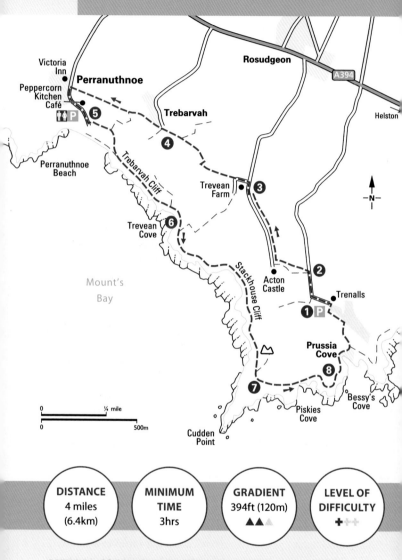

DISTANCE	MINIMUM TIME	GRADIENT	LEVEL OF DIFFICULTY
4 miles (6.4km)	3hrs	394ft (120m) ▲▲△	✚✚✚

PATHS Good field paths and coastal paths, 18 stiles **LANDSCAPE** Quiet coast and countryside **SUGGESTED MAP** OS Explorer 102 Land's End **START/FINISH** Grid reference: SW 555283 **DOG FRIENDLINESS** Dogs on lead through grazed areas **PARKING** Trenalls, Prussia Cove. Small, privately owned car park. Or car park at Perranuthnoe, from where the walk can be started at Point ⑤ **PUBLIC TOILETS** Perranuthnoe

WALK 34 DIRECTIONS

❶ From the Trennalls car park entrance walk back along the approach road, past the large house. Keep left and round the next sharp right-hand bend. Watch out for traffic. In about 150yds (137m), just past a field gate, walk through a hidden gap on the left, and into a field.

❷ Follow the field-edge, bearing off to the right, where it bends left, to reach a stile by a telegraph pole in the hedge opposite. Walk down the edge of the next field, behind the privately owned Acton Castle. Turn right and follow the bottom field-edge to its end. Go over a stile and follow the next field-edge to an overgrown stile. Cross this and then, half-way along the next field, go left over a stile and turn right along a lane.

❸ Turn left along a rough track at a junction in front of a bungalow entrance at Trevean Farm. In 55yds (50m) by Trevean House keep right, up a stony track, then go through a gate on the right. Follow the left-hand edge of a long field to a stile on its top edge, then follow the right-hand edge of the next field.

❹ At Trebarvah go over a stile and then through a gate. Cross a lane and continue across a stony area with houses on your right, (view of St Michael's Mount ahead), then follow a field-edge to a hedged-in path. Follow the path ahead through fields, then pass in front of some houses to reach the main road opposite the Victoria Inn. Go left and follow the road to the car park above Perranuthnoe Beach.

❺ For the beach and Cabin Café keep straight ahead. On the main route of the walk, go left, just beyond the car park, and along a lane. Bear right at a fork, then bear right again just past a house at a junction. Go down a track towards the sea and follow it round left. Then, at a field entrance, go down right (signposted), turn sharp left through a gap and follow a broad track.

❻ At a junction above Trevean Cove, bear off right from the track and then join a path to walk along the cliff edge.

❼ At the National Trust property of Cudden Point, follow the path steeply uphill and then across the inner slope of the headland above Piskies Cove.

❽ Go through a gate and pass some ancient fishing huts. Follow the path round the edge of the Bessy's Cove inlet of Prussia Cove, and go up some steps to reach a track by a thatched cottage. Bessy's Cove can be reached down a path on the right just before this junction. Turn right and follow the track, past a post box. Keep left at junctions, to return to the car park. Just before the car park is the Peppercorn Kitchen Café, noted for its tasty dishes and cakes (open all year).

ZENNOR'S DRAMATIC COAST AND COUNTRY

A varied walk along a spectacular coast
and through ancient field systems.

The Zennor area of West Cornwall is famous among visitors not least for an enduring local legend of a mermaid who was so enamoured of the singing of a local youth that she enticed him into the waters of Pendour Cove. This walk takes you along the cliffs above the cove, where you should keep your eyes open for the heads of seals rather than of mermaids.

Iron Age

This coastal shelf is barely a mile (1.6km) wide. It represents a classic example of a wave-cut platform that once lay beneath the sea and was later left high and dry as sea levels fell. The hills above Zennor are studded with huge granite slabs and rocks and in the small flat fields around the village you can see the rounded tops of massive boulders protruding from the grass. The boundaries of these field were first formed during the Iron Age and the granite 'hedges' that still separate the fields today create the random web-like pattern that makes the area so distinctive. Somewhere beneath the coastal fields lies the boundary between the moorland granite and the more ancient rocks of the nearby coast, the greenstone and slate that make up the dramatic coal-black cliffs that rise for over 200ft (61m) from the restless sea.

Mermaid's Lair

The lane from Zennor meets the coastal footpath that runs west along the rim of the cliffs above the mermaid's infamous lair of Pendour Cove. The coast path initially drops steeply into a narrow ravine cut by a bubbling stream that drains the moors and fields before tumbling over its boulder-strewn bed to the sea. From the high ground west of Pendour you can see the cliffs of Zennor Head across the bay, their walls jet black in colour and mottled with patches of green lichen. The path wriggles its way along the cliff top to the lesser headland of Carnelloe from where the walk leads inland and then back to Zennor along an ancient field path. At the end of the walk a visit to Zennor's Wayside Museum and Trewey Watermill fills in the social and cultural history of this remarkable landscape.

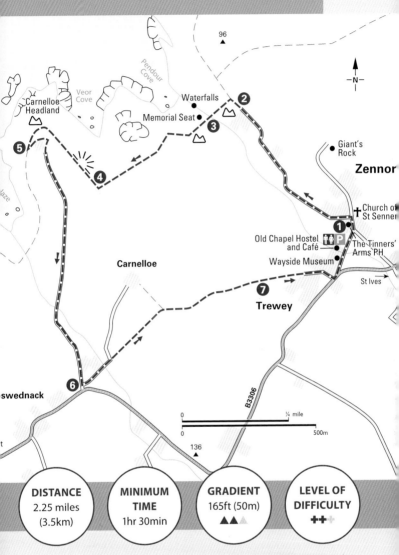

DISTANCE	MINIMUM TIME	GRADIENT	LEVEL OF DIFFICULTY
2.25 miles (3.5km)	1hr 30min	165ft (50m) ▲▲▲	✚✚✚

PATHS Occasionally rocky on coast path. Some steep steps to descend (handrails). Paths can be muddy after rain; 11 stiles

LANDSCAPE Rugged coast and small fields below rocky moorland

SUGGESTED MAP OS Explorer 102 Land's End

START/FINISH Grid reference: SW 454385

DOG FRIENDLINESS On lead through fields

PARKING Zennor car park (fee) **PUBLIC TOILETS** Beside car park

WALK 35 DIRECTIONS

1 Turn left out of the car park, pass The Tinners' Arms, turn left again and bear round left down a lane behind the pub. (The lane can be reached from the inner car park by going up right to a gate into the lane, then turning left.) Follow the lane for just over 0.5 miles (800m) to where it ends by an entrance to a house.

2 Keep straight ahead down a path for about 60yds (55m), cross a stile and turn left at a junction with the coast path. Descend quite steeply and, just by a bench, descend steep steps (handrail). Descend a final flight of steps to a wooden bridge across a stream that gushes over boulders to Pendour Cove below.

3 Follow the rocky path steeply uphill, and pass a memorial seat to the author Denys Val Baker. Continue uphill, ignoring a minor path going off right.

🍴 EATING AND DRINKING

The Tinners' Arms at Zennor is a famous institution and sits happily, and with due respect, below the village's other loftier edifice, the Church of St Senner. It's a mere skip and a jump between the two, in fact and Zennor has a grand sense of community. The Tinners' has a restaurant and lovely garden area and does pub food. Just by the car park is the cheerful Old Chapel Hostel and Café offering hot drinks, soup, baguettes, paninis and salads.

The path levels off above Veor Cove and a sweep of overgrown hillocks and hollows, relics of 19th-century mining.

4 Cross a stile and soon start to descend the north-east side of Carnelloe Headland; there are views to the cliffs of Zennor Head. Follow the path round the base of the headland and turn steeply uphill opposite some distinctive rock pinnacles.

5 Turn left at a junction below a house and climb steadily uphill. Follow the footpath behind the house to reach an open grassy area. Join a wide grassy track and follow it inland, passing a mine wheelpit down the slope on the right. Reach a junction by a stream. Cross a stone stile beside a wooden gate and keep left along a track.

6 Just before the main road, go left along a track in front of houses. Cross a bridge over a stream and in about 30yds (27m), bear off the track towards a metal gate and cross a granite stile on its left. Follow the left edge of a field and continue through several fields and over stiles.

7 Cross the final field and go over a stile and along a path beyond a muddy cattle track. Cross a stile, turn right down a lane and turn right along a concrete track through Trewey Farm. At the main road turn left, with care, and in a few paces, at a junction, keep left and steeply downhill to the car park.

ANCIENT STONES ON MADRON MOOR

A journey through a haunting landscape
of prehistoric antiquities and Victorian tin mines.

This moorland walk first takes you to a popular Bronze Age site known as the Mên-an-tol, or Stone of the Hole in prosaic English. This is an alignment of three granite stones comprising two short uprights to either side of a distinctive round stone pierced by a large hole. It was once known as 'The Crickstone' due to the claim that by crawling through it 'cricks' or aches in the back and neck could be cured. Another claim was that infants who were passed through the stone would be cured of rickets. There are many other fanciful associations, from the Druidic to modern 'white' witchcraftery. Enthusiasts still gather at propitious times of the year to commune. The reality is that the Mên-an-tol is probably the vestigial remnant of a neolithic-Bronze Age burial chamber or other site, the stones of which were later recycled for buildings elsewhere. According to records the present stones have been moved and realigned in historical times. It's perhaps best to wonder about them rather than to worship them.

Engine House

Beyond the Mên-an-tol, your path leads to the massive granite engine house of the Greenburrow mine shaft, part of a Victorian tin mine with the cheerful name of Ding Dong. It was so called because of the large bell that was rung to summon the miners to work. Greenburrow contained a huge steam powered beam engine that operated a pumping system to clear water from deep workings. From here a path leads to the Four Parishes Stone, a granite 'whaleback' boulder half buried in the ground that stands at the juncture of the old local parishes of Morvah, Zennor, Madron and Gulval. Even now, the features of this walk are not exhausted. The broad track that takes you back to the car park passes a permissive path that leads you to a single standing stone at the centre of a field. This is the Men Scryfa, the 'written stone'. It is particularly remarkable because of the inscription carved into its surface. This reads 'Rialobrani Cvnovali Fili' and is probably a form of dog Latin, in use during the late 5th and early 6th century AD. A suggested translation is 'Royal Raven, son of Famous Hound', referring, possibly, to post-Roman local leaders.

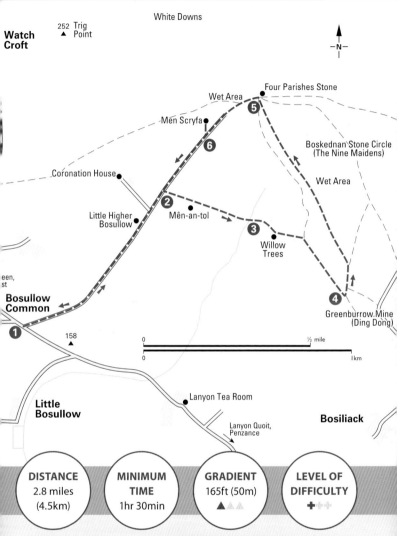

White Downs

Watch Croft

252 ▲ Trig Point

→N→

Four Parishes Stone

Wet Area

5

Mên Scryfa

6

Boskednan Stone Circle (The Nine Maidens)

Coronation House

Wet Area

2

Little Higher Bosullow

Mên-an-tol

3

Willow Trees

een, st

Bosullow Common

1

158 ▲

4

Greenburrow Mine (Ding Dong)

0 ·········· ½ mile

0 ·········· 1km

Little Bosullow

Lanyon Tea Room

Bosiliack

Lanyon Quoit, Penzance

DISTANCE	MINIMUM TIME	GRADIENT	LEVEL OF DIFFICULTY
2.8 miles (4.5km)	1hr 30min	165ft (50m) ▲▲▲	+++

PATHS Well-defined, but very wet and muddy underfoot after prolonged rain and generally so in winter **LANDSCAPE** Wild, undulating heathland with a great sense of openness **SUGGESTED MAP** OS Explorer 102 Land's End **START/FINISH** Grid reference: SW 418344 **DOG FRIENDLINESS** Cattle may be grazed on the open heathland at certain times. Dogs should be kept under strict control **PARKING** Roadside parking opposite a house with '1882' on its gable. Please do not obstruct the gate across the access track **PUBLIC TOILETS** None on route

Opposite: Ancient standing stone, Mên-an-tol

WALK 36 DIRECTIONS

❶ From the parking area, go through a metal side gate, next to a larger gate and follow a broad stony track between high granite hedges. In about 0.5 miles (800m), pass the ruined buildings of Little Higher Bosullow on the left with the isolated Coronation House two fields above.

❷ Turn off right over a small slab bridge and a granite stile and then follow the grassy path to the stones of the Mên-an-tol. Keep straight on to the left of the Mên-an-tol and follow the continuation path to reach a small stream. (This can be crossed by a fairly long stride or by getting your boots momentarily wet.)

❸ Continue uphill through willows and reach a gateway. Ahead is the tall building and Greenburrow Mine.

❹ Turn left at a junction of paths just before Greenburrow Mine stack. Keep left at the next junction and follow a path across the moor to a junction of paths beside the Four Parishes Stone. The obvious path that leads east and uphill from the Four Parishes Stone

> ### ☙ IN THE AREA
> Just under 1 mile (1.6km) along the road to Madron from the parking area is the ancient monument of Lanyon Quoit, a huge granite slab perched on three upright stone pillars. It represents the bare bones of a Late Neolithic-Early Bronze Age tomb, probably of a local leader.

leads to the late neolithic-early Bronze Age stone circle of Boskednan, known also as The Nine Maidens.

❺ On the main route turn left at the Four Parishes Stone and go through a wide gap. Follow a broad grassy track, keep left at an indeterminate junction and follow a narrower track between banks and stone hedges. This is often very wet and muddy. There are several escape routes over the bank on the left to a drier, parallel path.

❻ Where the track widens go over a steep stone stile on the right and visit the Men Scryfa stone. Return to the lane and turn right, eventually passing the access stile to the Mên-an-tol used previously. Continue down the lane to the parking area.

> ### ☙ EATING AND DRINKING
> The Lanyon Tea Room is located about 0.25 miles (400m) from the car parking area on the road towards Lanyon Quoit and Madron. You can enjoy cream teas and cakes as well as hot and cold drinks and ice cream. At Pendeen on the north coast B3306 main road there are two pubs where you can get snacks and meals. Pendeen is about 3 miles (4.8km) west of the start of this walk.

HIDDEN CORNERS OF HISTORIC PENZANCE

A gentle stroll through
a famous Cornish town.

There is a Mediterranean ring to the name Penzance that goes well with the town's sunny south-facing aspect on the shores of Mount's Bay, one of the largest bays in Britain. This is a town whose mellow climate even encourages the growth of palm trees and where you really do have a sense of being almost 'abroad'.

Ancient Chapel

Penzance was made a borough as early as 1614 and received an even greater economic boost in the later 17th century when it became a 'Stannary' or 'Coinage' town with the right to assay and tax tin and copper from the many mines on the Land's End peninsula. The town reached its commercial apogee in the 19th century when many of the fine buildings seen on this walk were built. Penzance shares in the artistic heritage of West Cornwall. Nearby Newlyn saw the late 19th-century emergence of the Newlyn School of Painting. This was the label given to a style, based on the French *'plein air'* or 'open air' tradition, by which artists painted out of doors in a more dynamic and immediate fashion. During the walk you pass the Penlee House Gallery and Museum, which has a collection of Newlyn School paintings.

Regency Period

The finest buildings in Penzance date from the Regency period and its immediate aftermath. Regent Square, through which your route passes, is a splendid example. The town also has a legacy of fine open spaces, such as the Morrab Gardens, which evolved during the same period. There are many more architectural gems. During the first part of the walk you pass the 1930s art deco swimming lido, known as the Jubilee Pool and the nearby Yacht Inn, a classic of 20th-century marine architecture. The walk then leads to Chapel Street, Penzance's finest thoroughfare, which has a mix of styles and boasts the one-time home of Maria Branwell, the mother of the famous Brontë sisters. Ultra modern style is represented at The Exchange art gallery while Penzance's Market Jew Street brings you back to the busy commercial town.

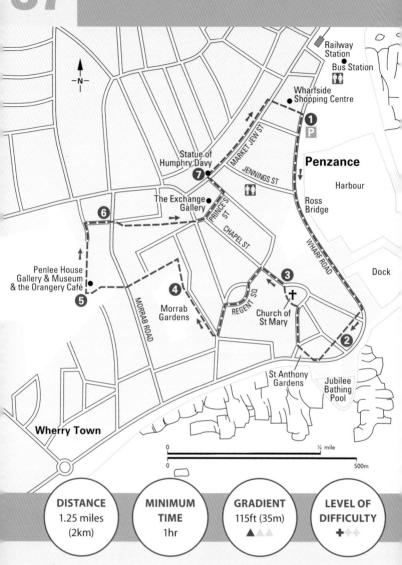

WALK 37 DIRECTIONS

1 Exit the Harbour Car Park on to Wharf Road and cross the road using the pedestrian crossing in front of the Wharfside Shopping Centre. Turn left and pass the old Lifeboat Station, cross the junction and continue across Ross Bridge. Bear right in front of The Dolphin Tavern and go up the cobbled lane to the right of the pub.

2 Cross a junction, slightly leftwards, to the seafront road. In a few paces turn right into the peaceful St Anthony Gardens. Walk through the gardens and exit in the far left-hand corner opposite The Yacht Inn. Cross left to South Place. Turn right and climb steps beneath a granite archway into St Mary's churchyard. Climb more steps and continue into Chapel Street.

3 Turn left then left again opposite The Admiral Benbow pub and into Voundervour Lane. Keep left at the next junction and go through Regent Square. On leaving the square, cross the road, turn left and, in a few paces, turn right. Go through a gap in railings just beyond a line of lock-up garages. Turn right and enter Morrab Gardens.

4 Leave by the gate in the top right-hand corner of the gardens. After about 30yds (27m) go left down an alleyway in front of a terrace of handsome houses. Keep straight ahead across a junction of lanes and across a pedestrian crossing in Morrab Road.

> ### 🍴 EATING AND DRINKING
> The Orangery Café at the Penlee House Gallery and Museum does delicious food in a lovely setting and is licensed. You pass a number of public houses on the walk and all serve snacks and pub lunches.

Turn right and in a few paces go left through the gates of Penlee Park.

5 Just past the Penlee House Gallery and Museum turn right along a leafy walkway. Mid-way along visit the Memorial Garden on the right. On the main route keep straight ahead and follow the walkway round to the right. Go through a gateway and keep uphill to reach Morrab Road.

6 Cross the road (with care) and go along an alleyway between houses. At a junction of lanes keep straight across. At the next junction, by The Globe public house, cross the street, turn right and in a few paces turn left along Prince's Street past The Exchange Art Gallery. Turn left at the next junction to reach Market Jew Street.

7 Cross the street and go up steps behind the statue of Humphry Davy, inventor of the miner's safety lamp. Turn right down The Terrace, a raised, granite walkway. When opposite the Wharfside Shopping Centre, cross the street, go through the centre and down the escalator to the Harbour car park.

LAMORNA'S GRANITE COAST AND COUNTRY

Golden granite, green fields and the ever-changing sea create a rich palette of Cornish colours.

Lamorna Cove has long been a popular tourist destination, but the area once resonated with the clang of hammers and the roar of explosions from quarrying. Granite from Lamorna was used in the Thames Embankment, New Scotland Yard and in various lighthouses, including the Longships Lighthouse off Land's End. The most dramatic relics of quarrying at Lamorna are the large heaps of granite on the northern slopes of the cove and the quarry above.

The first stage of this walk winds its way uphill through the old quarry landscape, now softened by a green pelt of trees that smothers the slopes of the Lamorna Valley. You follow in the ghostly trail of horses that once hauled wagons, laden with huge blocks of granite, up to the high ground and on to Penzance. Soon the quarry track is abandoned for a field path that links a trio of typical Cornish farms where you first meet the granite stiles and famous field 'hedges' of Cornwall, in reality double-skinned stone walls smothered with vegetation. The way leads to the farm settlements of Kemyel Crease and Kemyel Drea, where you get close to the healthy odours of a working farm as the path leads through the heart of the cow yards.

To the Coast

Soon the fields lead down to the coast path and the way back to Lamorna. Look out for the disused and overgrown coastguard lookout at Penzer Point where a constant watch was once kept on the local fishing fleet and on passing shipping. This offical service has been terminated and many local fishing boats now have on-board satellite navigation systems and ship-to-shore radios. Wrecks can still occur on this rugged coast, however, when the sea is in the mood for mayhem and the wind is wild. Yet the sunblessed slopes here were once cultivated for the growing of early flowers and potatoes in tiny sheltered meadows called quillets, some of which are still in use. From Penzer Point the path descends steeply and then passes through Kemyel Crease Wood, a deep stand of mainly Monterey pines and cypresses that was savagely thinned out by a huge storm in 1990. Beyond the trees the breezy coastline is followed past granite slabs and boulders back to Lamorna Cove.

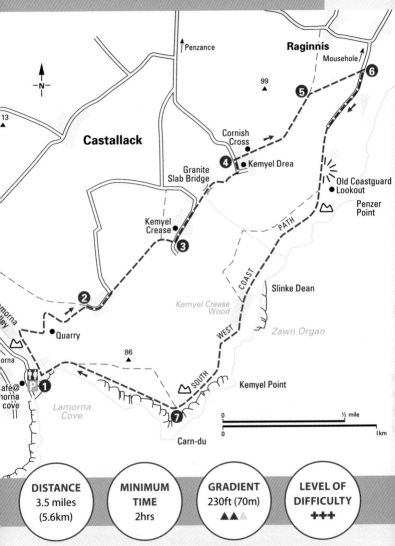

DISTANCE	MINIMUM TIME	GRADIENT	LEVEL OF DIFFICULTY
3.5 miles (5.6km)	2hrs	230ft (70m) ▲▲▲	+++

PATHS Well-defined coastal footpath. Field paths are not so well defined;
15 stiles, most of which are high; inland paths can be very wet after prolonged
rain and in winter **LANDSCAPE** Rocky coastal landscape and higher, inland fields
with panoramic views **SUGGESTED MAP** OS Explorer 102 Land's End
START/FINISH Grid reference: SW 451241 **DOG FRIENDLINESS** Dogs should be
on lead within the Lamorna Cove area and under strict control on field sections
and farm areas; small dogs may find the high stiles difficult **PARKING** Lamorna
Cove car park (fee) **PUBLIC TOILETS** Lamorna Cove

Lamorna Cove

WALK 38 DIRECTIONS

❶ Turn right out of the car park and walk in front of a row of cottages. Cross a bridge over a river, bear right and round left and, in a few paces, turn left at a junction. Follow a narrow path that zig-zags uphill among trees. Pass an overgrown quarry and continue uphill on the main path to reach a junction at Kemyel Wartha.

❷ Turn right and follow a stony track between the houses. At a left-hand bend, go over a steep stile on the right. Follow the field-edge to a stile and then go straight across the next field to a stile. Follow the next field-edge and, where it bends left, keep straight ahead and reach a stile into a lane at Kemyel Crease.

ⓨ EATING AND DRINKING

There is a licensed café-restaurant at Lamorna Cove called café@lamorna cove (but you don't have to email them beforehand). The café is open all day and offers breakfast, lunch and evening meals as well as cream teas and snacks. Just over 0.5 miles (800m) up the narrow approach road to the cove is Lamorna Wink pub, which serves pub meals and snacks.

---

❸ Turn left and follow a surfaced road between houses. Just before an isolated house, go right and over a low stile. Turn left down the edge of a meadow to cross a stile into an area of boggy woodland. Follow the path

across a bridge of huge granite slabs and continue to farm buildings at Kemyel Drea.

❹ Go through a gate at a halfway point in the farm buildings. Continue through several gates and across cow yards to reach a stile beside a small Cornish cross. Follow the left edges of the next three fields, crossing high stiles between each one. There is a granite rubbing post in the third, narrowest field.

❺ In the next field ignore the stile directly opposite and instead, go diagonally right across the field to a stile, two thirds of the way down the opposite hedge. In the next field, head diagonally right towards a house and cross a stile in the hedge. Turn right down a narrow path.

❻ At a junction turn right onto the coast path. Just beyond a redundant and overgrown coastguard lookout, descend very steep steps almost to sea level. Follow the path as it winds across some rocky sections to enter Kemyel Crease Wood. Go through the wood and then follow the coast path just above the sea

❼ Climb steep steps to the rocky point of Carn-du, and then descend more steps and follow the path across several rocky, but safe, sections to reach Lamorna Cove and the start of the walk.

CAPE CORNWALL'S MINING HINTERLAND

A coast and countryside walk through the St Just
and Cape Cornwall Mining World Heritage Site.

St Just and Cape Cornwall were once at the heart of Cornwall's dramatic tin
and copper mining industry. Mining has now ceased, but the history of St Just
mining is of such significance that the area is now a part of the Devon and
Cornwall World Heritage Mining Site. The coastal cliffs of Cape Cornwall are
not composed of the golden granite that so distinguishes much of the Land's
End peninsula. They comprise more ancient rocks, known as 'country rock',
the primeval sedimentary shales that were later transformed and 'baked' by
the molten granite that erupted from deep within the earth. The intense heat,
the chemical reactions and the physical changes that took place produced
the abundant mineral deposits that made West Cornwall famous.

During the heyday of Victorian mining, the St Just area was a vibrant, if
bleak, industrial landscape with over 2,000 people employed in mining below
and above ground. Today, much of the detritus and perishable structures of
all this industry are now gone or buried beneath vegetation. What survives
are the granite chimneystacks, buildings, wheel pits and water leats of the
mine processing works that once filled the valleys and cliffside with noise and
fury and swirling clouds of smoke and dust.

Brutal Reality

Amid all of this, men, women and children worked endlessly in one of the
toughest environments ever. We marvel at the romance of it all, but the reality
was often brutal. Mineral ores were rich in arsenic and the 'calciner' building
past which this walk leads, was used to extract arsenic from raw ore at times
when tin was unprofitable. Arsenic commanded good prices as a pesticide
against the boll weevil in the American cotton fields. The ore was 'baked' in
the calciners and the smoke drafted through labyrinthine tunnels. The arsenic
and other chemicals were deposited as powder on the tunnel walls. This
was then scraped off, mainly by women and young boys whose lungs and
skin were unprotected. Life expectancy for the arsenic harvesters was slight.
In many ways, the evocative ruins around Cape Cornwall serve as powerful
memorials to a dramatic industry and to a remarkable people.

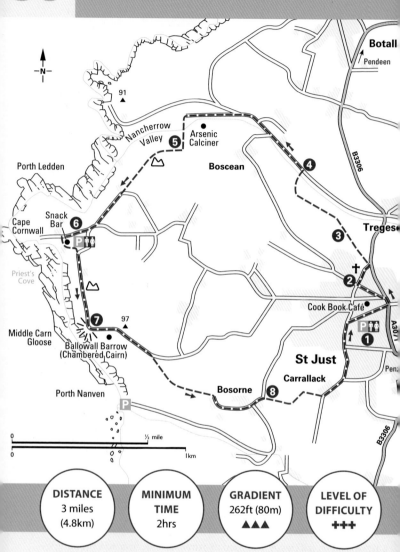

DISTANCE	MINIMUM TIME	GRADIENT	LEVEL OF DIFFICULTY
3 miles (4.8km)	2hrs	262ft (80m) ▲▲▲	+++

PATHS Mostly well defined; some coastal sections steep and rocky; wet and muddy underfoot after prolonged rain; 9 stiles **LANDSCAPE** Coastal area with industrial archaeology **SUGGESTED MAP** OS Explorer 102 Land's End **START/FINISH** Grid reference: SW 369313 **DOG FRIENDLINESS** Dogs on lead in field sections where there may be livestock **PARKING** St Just free car park opposite the St Just Library **PUBLIC TOILETS** St Just car park and Cape Cornwall car park **NOTE** The walk can be started either from St Just car park or from the National Trust car park at Cape Cornwall where there is a fee for non-NT members

WALK 39 DIRECTIONS

❶ Leave the car park and turn right, opposite the library, to reach Market Square. Turn left and pass a clock tower on your left. At the road junction go straight across (with care). Do not continue along the main road, but take the narrow Chapel Street, to its left.

❷ At a T-junction, with the Wesleyan chapel opposite, turn right and at a junction with the main road, by a public footpath sign, go left along a narrow passageway in front of two cottages. Go over a stile and cross a small field to a stile. Go diagonally right across the next field toward three telegraph poles.

❸ Go over a stile, bear round left and alongside the field-edge to another stile. Follow the path between trees; go over a stile and cross a road at a waste water plant. Go over a stile and a footbridge to a surfaced lane running down the Nancherrow Valley, also known as the Kenidjack Valley.

❹ Turn left along the lane. Keep ahead onto a rough track at a junction by a house. At the next junction keep right along the track and at the next junction take the left-hand branch downhill. Turn left at Coast Path signs along a narrow path and across a footbridge.

❺ Follow the path as it winds steeply uphill. Keep right where it begins to level off at a junction. Keep right at

> 🍴 **EATING AND DRINKING**
> The Cook Book Café at 4 Cape Cornwall Street, St Just is just down from the clock tower and has a terrific collection of over 5,000 second-hand books. The food is excellent also. There are also several pubs in St Just serving bar food.

the next junction and reach a surfaced road above Cape Cornwall.

❻ Follow the road down right past a National Trust car park. Turn sharp left at a gateway to a private road and go down a series of granite steps. Turn left up a steep surfaced lane at a junction above Priest's Cove. Turn sharply right at the next junction and follow a stony track uphill to Middle Carn Gloose.

❼ Follow a surfaced road past the Ballowall Barrow Bronze Age grave. Turn right down a track about 50yds (46m) beyond a mine stack and opposite a bench. Keep straight ahead across two junctions to a surfaced road that leads between houses. Cross a broad junction and go up the lane opposite for 50yds (46m).

❽ Turn right in front of a house and go through a kissing gate. Follow an overgrown path to a stile. Cross a field to a stile. Turn left along the field edge. Go over a stile at buildings to reach a lane. Turn left, keep left at the next junction, and at a third junction, turn right to the car park.

GOLDEN BEACHES AND CLIFFS AT PORTHCURNO

Along interlocking footpaths between sandy coves and granite cliffs on the Land's End peninsula.

Land's End may be the ultimate visitor destination in Cornwall. It is the most westerly point certainly and its cliffs are spectacular; but for the true aficionado of coastal scenery, the granite cliffs of Porthcurno and Porthgwarra, to the south of Land's End, are hard to beat for their beauty and sculpted forms.

Golden Sand

This walk starts at Porthcurno, where a sweeping expanse of golden shell sand lies at the heart of an arc of granite cliffs that embrace the small bay. On the south side lies the rocky coxcomb of Treryn Dinas, or Logan Rock. To the north is the famous Minack Open Air Theatre, built within the rocky ribs of the headland. The final section of the walk passes the Minack, but first the route leads inland and across fields to the splendid little Church of St Levan, couched in one of the few sheltered spots on this robust coast.

Below the church a shallow valley runs down to Porth Chapel Beach, more besieged by tides than Porthcurno, but still a delightful place, especially in summer. Again the beach here is left for later in the walk, whose route now leads along the coast path and then climbs inland before dropping down to Porthgwarra Cove, where tunnels and caverns in the cliff were carved out by farmers and fishermen to give better access to the narrow beach. From Porthgwarra, you head back along the coast path to Porth Chapel. The path leads you down past the little Well of St Levan. Below here there is a rocky access path to the beach.

Spectacular Steps

The route of the walk leads steeply up to Rospletha Point and then to the remarkable cliff face theatre at Minack. From here, the most direct way down to Porthcurno Beach is by a series of very steep steps that may not suit everyone. But if you don't mind the vertiginous experience, the views really are outstanding. You can avoid this descent by some judicious road walking. Either way Porthcurno's glorious beach is at hand in the cove below you.

Opposite: The Minack Theatre at Porthcurno

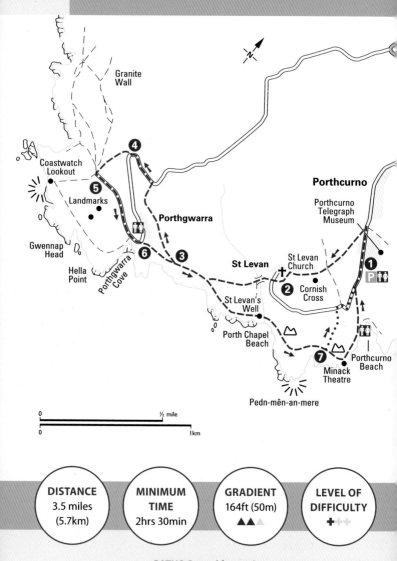

DISTANCE	MINIMUM TIME	GRADIENT	LEVEL OF DIFFICULTY
3.5 miles (5.7km)	2hrs 30min	164ft (50m) ▲▲△	✚✚✚

PATHS Coastal footpath

LANDSCAPE Granite sea cliffs and inland fields and heath

SUGGESTED MAP OS Explorer 102 Land's End

START/FINISH Grid reference: SW 384224

DOG FRIENDLINESS Dogs should be kept under control on beach and fields

PARKING Porthcurno and Porthgwarra

PUBLIC TOILETS Porthgwarra and Porthcurno

WALK 40 DIRECTIONS

❶ From Porthcurno car park, walk back up the approach road, then just before Sea View House, turn sharply left along a track and follow it to reach cottages. Pass to the right of the cottages and turn right through a gap. Follow a field path past a granite cross and go through a wooden gate.

❷ Enter St Levan churchyard by a granite stile. Go round the far side of the church to the entrance gate and on to a surfaced lane. Cross the lane and follow the path opposite, signed to Porthgwarra Cove. Cross a footbridge then in about 55yds (50m), at a junction, take the right fork and follow the path to merge with the main coast path and keep ahead.

🍴 EATING AND DRINKING

There is a seasonal café at Porthgwarra, located mid-way in the walk. Porthcurno has several outlets including the Beach Café and the Cable Station Inn. A seasonal ice cream and soft drinks van is usually located in the Porthcurno car park.

---

❸ Where the path begins to descend towards Porthgwarra Cove, branch off right up some wooden steps. Reach a surfaced track by a house and turn up right, then at a road, turn left.

❹ Go round a sharp left-hand bend, then at a footpath signpost, go right down a grassy path and cross a stone footbridge. Continue uphill to reach a bend on a track, just up from large granite houses.

❺ Turn left, go over a stile beside a gate, then continue down a surfaced lane to Porthgwarra Cove. Just past the shop and café, and opposite a red telephone box, go right down a track, signposted 'Coast Path', then follow the path round left. Just past a house, go sharp right at a junction and climb up the steps.

❻ Follow the coast path, partly reversing the ongoing route. Keep right at a junction, and eventually descend past St Levan's Well to just above Porth Chapel Beach. (Dogs should be on a lead.) Follow the coast path steeply over Pedn-mên-an-mere, and continue to the Minack Theatre car park.

❼ For the surefooted, cross the car park and go down the track to the left of the Minack complex, then descend the steep cliff steps, with great care. When the path levels off, continue to a junction. The right fork takes you to Porthcurno Beach and the car park. The continuation leads to the road by the Beach Café, where a right turn leads to the car park. A less challenging alternative to the cliff steps is to turn left out of the Minack car park. Follow the approach road to a T-junction with a public road. Turn right, watching out for traffic and follow the road downhill to the car park.

Walking in Safety

All these walks are suitable for any reasonably fit person, but less experienced walkers should try the easier walks first. Route finding is usually straightforward, but you will find that an Ordnance Survey map is a useful addition to the route maps and descriptions.

RISKS

Although each walk here has been researched with a view to minimising the risks to the walkers who follow its route, no walk in the countryside can be considered to be completely free from risk. Walking in the outdoors will always require a degree of common sense and judgement to ensure that it is as safe as possible.

- Be particularly careful on cliff paths and in upland terrain, where the consequences of a slip can be very serious.
- Remember to check tidal conditions before walking on the seashore.
- Some sections of route are by, or cross, busy roads. Take care and remember traffic is a danger even on minor country lanes.
- Be careful around farmyard machinery and livestock, especially if you have children with you.
- Be aware of the consequences of changes in the weather and check the forecast before you set out. Carry spare clothing and a torch if you are walking in the winter months. Remember the weather can change very quickly at any time of the year, and in moorland and heathland areas, mist and fog can make route finding much harder. Don't set out in these conditions unless you are confident of your navigation skills in poor visibility. In summer remember to take account of the heat and sun; wear a hat and carry spare water.

On walks away from centres of population you should carry a whistle and survival bag. If you do have an accident requiring the emergency services, make a note of your position as accurately as possible and dial 999.

COUNTRYSIDE CODE

- Be safe, plan ahead and follow any signs.
- Leave gates and property as you find them.
- Protect plants and animals and take your litter home.
- Keep dogs under close control.
- Consider other people.

For more information on the Countryside Code visit:
www.naturalengland.org.uk/ourwork/enjoying/countrysidecode